Getting Ready to Help

A Primer on Interacting in Human Service

by

Martin J. McMorrow
Proactive Behavioral Design, Inc.
Cobden, Illinois

·P·A·U·L·H·
BROOKES
PUBLISHING C○ ®

Baltimore • London • Sydney

Paul H. Brookes Publishing Co.
Post Office Box 10624
Baltimore, Maryland 21285-0624

www.brookespublishing.com

Typeset by International Graphic Services, Inc., Newtown, Pennsylvania.
Manufactured in the United States of America by
Versa Press, East Peoria, Illinois.

All case studies in this book are based on the author's actual experiences. In all instances, names have been changed; in some instances, identifying details have been altered to further protect confidentiality.

Cover photographs by Keith Cotton of Photography by Keith Cotton, 102 South Front Street, Cobden, Illinois 62920-0152.

A package of five copies of this book is available at a discounted price. Contact the publisher at 1-800-638-3775 for more information.

Library of Congress Cataloging-in-Publication Data

McMorrow, Martin J.
  Getting ready to help : A primer on interacting in human service / by
    Martin J. McMorrow.
      p.   cm.
  Includes bibliographical references.
  ISBN 1-55766-612-1
  1. Therapist and patient.   2. Helping behavior.   3. Psychiatric social
    work.   I. Title.

RC480.8 .M395   2002
616.89'14—dc21   2002034238

British Library Cataloguing in Publication data are available from the
British Library.

Contents

☐ ☐ ☐ ☐ ☐ ☐

About the Author

Martin J. McMorrow, M.S., received his degree in behavior analysis and therapy from Southern Illinois University. He recently started a staff training and consulting company called Proactive Behavioral Design, Inc., and is Coordinator of Strategic Development and Growth at the Center for Comprehensive Services (CCS) in Carbondale, Illinois, which is part of the National Mentor ABI Network. Marty co-developed the social skills training program *Stacking the Deck,* the language training program *Looking for the Words,* and numerous other behavioral clinical interventions with his colleagues at the Behavior Research Lab at the Anna Mental Health and Developmental Center. He also led the design, implementation, and evaluation of the Personal Intervention Neurobehavioral Rehabilitation Program at CCS. Having had numerous opportunities to interact with people with developmental disabilities, mental illness, and acquired brain injuries, Marty's primary interest is in translating behavioral technology into proactive and applicable interactions that will make a difference in the lives of both the people being helped and the people doing the helping—the subject matter of this book.

Foreword

Marty McMorrow has given us a great gift by providing this handbook. By tracing his own professional development, his successes and failures in "helping," he allows us to more quickly find the joy in helping. Those working in human and social services and the criminal justice system as well as policy makers should read and reread this book to understand the essentials of human interaction and relationships.

The underlying theory in Marty's work is that all behavior is purposeful and adaptive for the person engaging in the behavior. He shows us through wonderful, and sometimes painful, examples that helping is not about power, control, submission, or compliance—that helping requires real work by the helper. Helping is also about looking for the gifts and capacities of individuals, as we learned from Dr. Herb Lovett. He teaches us that understanding behavior is often about common sense, which another applied behavior analyst, Dr. John McGee, the author of *Gentle Teaching,* said is "the least commonly used of all of the senses." Most important, Marty emphasizes that the roles of helper and helpee often change. When talking with people working in the field of traumatic brain injury, I frequently state, "Remember that you or one of your family members could be the person with the injury. How would you like to be approached if you were the person needing help?"

Marty advocates for providing proactive behavioral treatment in community integrated settings. As a result of the landmark U.S. Supreme Court decision in the case of *L.C. and E.W. v. Olmstead* in 1999, state and local government services to people with disabilities, as defined functionally under the Americans with Disabilities Act (ADA) of 1990, must be provided in the most integrated setting appropriate to the needs of the individual. The integration mandate asserts that all people with disabilities, regardless of severity, have a constitutionally protected civil right to live in the community with the appropriate services and supports. The challenge to us in the helping professions is to work with the individuals with disabilities and others to develop the services and supports to actualize that right. Marty gives us a map to this new destination, which requires each of us to search our own values and souls about why we do what we do.

Marty's values embrace the goals of the ADA: equality of opportunity, full participation, independent living, and economic self-sufficiency. His approach requires the helper to engage the person receiving the help in designing his or her own plan of interventions. This book celebrates the changes we have experienced in the evolution of disability services in the United States. We have finally moved away from a period dominated by large, congregate care, segregated institutions in which individuals with disabilities were treated as subhumans from 1848 to the 1970s. Since 1987, the terms "inclusion," "circles of support," "personal futures planning," and "self-determination" have moved into our work and rhetoric but not fully into our practice. It is within this paradigm that Marty's approach to reciprocity and the creation of mutually reinforcing relationships truly shines. We have moved into an era when we approach all people with respect and as equals in the diversity of the human condition.

Marty is a superb map drawer for the 21st century who conveys the essence of the joy of helping people to have a sense of belonging in our society. Thank you, Marty, for helping us see how to better travel the journey to an interdependent society in which all of us belong.

Allan I. Bergman
President & CEO
Brain Injury Association of America

Preface

I consider myself really fortunate to have been involved in human services since the 1970s. So very much has happened: exciting medical advances have improved the lives of some people considered to have mental illnesses, innovative teaching technologies have enhanced independence options for some people considered to have developmental disabilities, and new rehabilitation options have allowed some people with brain injuries to have their lives back after catastrophic accidents. In addition, more people in need of help are receiving it in their home communities, many new potential helpers have become involved, and there has been increased attention and sensitivity to the rights and preferences of many individuals who experience difficulties in their lives.

Yet, before anyone begins to think that everything is all figured out or that all of the good work has been done, perhaps it would be useful to look at a few other realities. For example, according to the Centers for Disease Control and Prevention (1999), 7.3 million people in the United States are considered to have developmental disabilities. There are 5.3 million others who are considered to have disabilities resulting from mental illness and another 5.3 million considered to have disabilities resulting from brain injuries experienced in automobile accidents, falls, assaults, and other unfortunate life events. And, of course, there are easily that many others whose daily challenges present huge emotional difficulties in their lives who are not considered to have disabilities. This is a great many people, and only a small percentage of them experience any medical advances, innovative teaching technologies, or new rehabilitation options that have affected their lives in important ways. Furthermore, many people in need of help continue to be excluded from their communities, many people who could be in a position to help still turn their backs, and many people continue to be mistreated or not treated at all on a regular basis.

No matter how much progress is made in human services, it is easy to be moved by how much has remained the same and how much there remains to do. As I have tried to narrow these issues down to determine how and what to communicate to people who may be getting ready to help, two issues have continued to stand out for me. First, although there seems to be plenty of good science and technology available that could help organize and drive the delivery of human services well into the future, my experience has been that there are rarely enough people who understand and agree on how these technologies might be used to make much of a difference in many human services situations. In addition, many direct care service providers, family members, and others who are often in the best position to help may have difficulty with finding, selecting, comprehending, and implementing many of the scientifically sound, yet very complicated, helping methods that exist. If we are going to extend useful help to more people, then these individuals need understandable and applicable methods that relate to the available technologies. Second, and even more important right now, many people who might be in a position to help (e.g., family members, some professionals, administrators, students) simply don't know where and how to get started in changing the outcomes of helping situations they may find themselves in.

The title of this book, *Getting Ready to Help: A Primer on Interacting in Human Service*, was chosen primarily to encourage consideration of issues that may guide helping efforts on behalf of others, before helpers actually engage in those activities. It implies that there are questions you can ask, decisions you can make, and things that you can do prior to becoming involved in a helping situation that may better prepare you for some of the incredible experiences you are likely to have after you get started. It rests on the assumption that the science, method, and technology of helping are fundamentally embedded in social interaction between people. Perhaps if helpers can gain a better understanding of those interactions, we can get ourselves in a better position to experience success in efforts on behalf of others and, as important, the joy that can be derived from serving others.

Why have you become involved in the first place? How can your interactions get you in a better position to help? Are there ways of interacting that may increase your chances for greater success? What's the purpose of helping anyway? How can you get greater satisfaction, excitement, or joy from helping so that you will be inclined to do more of it? Are there any ways of interacting that can make the residence, unit, classroom, home, community, or world a better place to be alive?

Because I have not seen these sorts of questions addressed in one place and because I have spent so much time with many wonderful people trying to find useful answers to these questions, I attempt in this book to communicate some of what I have learned. My intention is to share some ideas that may influence your thinking and doing within helping contexts. Some of these ideas are based on empirical support, and others are not. All of them are just reflections of everything that has gone before for me, in my experience, in my interpretation of that experience, in my life. I truly hope that they are useful in yours.

REFERENCE

Centers for Disease Control and Prevention. (1999). *Traumatic brain injury in the United States: A report to Congress.* Atlanta: Author.

Acknowledgments

I thank everyone who brought out the best in me, including my friends from High Hopes, the Clyde L. Choate Mental Health and Developmental Center, the Center for Comprehensive Services, the Caritas Peace Center, and everywhere else I have attempted to help. I acknowledge a few people I have only met—B.F. Skinner, Jon Bailey, Muhammad Ali—and several others with whom I have interacted much more—Nate Azrin, Reed Bechtel, Roger Poppen, Richard Foxx, Don Thomas, John Kirkpatrick, Gerry Faw, Kathy Fralish, Mary Kay Moore, Christopher Reed McMorrow, and Debra Braunling-McMorrow—for the various influences they have had on my life. Of course, there have been so many others.

To my father, Dr. Thomas McMorrow,
who has always been my primary model in helping.

I Could Have Been a Map Drawer

You just never know when you might get the opportunity to help someone. Although I remember being polite to kids who were seen as different when I was growing up, I never thought I would wind up spending so much time with people like them as part of my career. The beginning of my career happened very much by accident in 1971 after I left college early and found myself sitting in a military recruiting office. When the recruiter asked me what I wanted to do in the Army, I was surprised because I didn't think I would have that sort of a choice. I thought people would tell me what to do in the Army. I guess I thought I needed to be told what to do at that time in my life.

Anyway, when I looked at my "career choices" on the alphabetical list the recruiter showed me, my first selection was journalism. Could I be a journalist in the Army? That seemed pretty special, so I decided to make the request. The answer was "no." I somehow qualified to be a journalist, but the training was not available at that time. My second choice on the list was map drawing. I could draw maps in the Army? I knew I had no interest in hurting anyone. I had done a lot of drawing when I was younger, and I thought this would be harmless enough. Curiously, drawing maps was not available either. The recruiter told me to keep looking. I began to wonder if I really had a choice in the matter or if I was just being led down a particular path. I'm not sure it is a good thing to lead someone to believe they have a choice about something when it is clear that they really don't. As a result, for a few moments, I wasn't feeling too good about my future.

Then, as I looked on through the list of things that I might be doing for the next 3 years in the military, a life changing event occurred. Under the "P"s on the career list was something called "psychiatric/social work." I could be a psychiatric/social worker in the Army? With just 2 1/2 years of unrelated college courses behind me? Without much of a clue about where I was headed at that time in my life? Without having given the first thought to what helping people was really about? The recruiter's answer was "yes." I was soon on a bus to the Army to get healthy, get my 10 weeks of psychiatric/social work training, and get the opportunity to help others.

Perhaps this is the kind of situation that you are facing right now. Maybe someone is looking to you for help. Maybe you can see a situation in which your help is needed. Maybe you are about to respond to one of the many job opportunities related to helping others that are listed in your local newspaper. Maybe you have already been trying to help for some time, but you are discouraged because you don't feel like you are very good at it. Maybe others are telling you that you are not very good at it. Whatever the reason, I am happy that you have found your way to this book and that you may consider some of these ideas to help you get in a better position to help.

It has been more than 30 years since that choice showed up in my life. In fact, I am now one of those people who has spent most of my adult existence in situations in which people were either in need of help or actually wanted help from others: people with mental retardation, developmental disabilities, mental illness, physical disabilities, personality disorders, substance abuse, behavioral disturbances, autism, acquired and traumatic brain injuries, marital problems, emotional problems, orientation problems, bedwetting problems, personal problems, situational problems, problems, problems, and more problems. I have worked with people who seem to make very poor decisions, who hurt themselves, who hurt others, who make threats, who develop very unusual ways of acting, and who wind up in serious trouble. I met them in their homes, on the street, in various sorts of institutions, in group living residences, in classrooms, in hospitals, and in clinic offices.

Although there have been moments when I mistakenly began to believe that I knew everything I needed to know about helping, I have been repeatedly humbled by unpredicted successes and unfortunate failures that others perceived in their lives. For the most part, these experiences have just sparked my interest in continuing to learn. This book is intended to identify, describe, and share a few of the most important things I have learned about helping. These things have guided most of the decisions, recommendations, and choices I have made in my human service life. I thank all of the people who helped me learn them—usually the people I was trying to help or those who also attempted to help along with me. I wish I had known more of them when I started; if I had, I might have been a better helper, and I might have found even greater joy from my work.

But then, as life goes, I realize I could have been a map drawer.

Do No Harm

After completing 8 weeks of classroom training to become a military psychiatric social worker, it was time for my first real-life interaction with someone who was clearly in need of help. I was told to report to an Army hospital psychiatric unit where I would meet with other psychiatric social workers who would supervise this hands-on part of my training.

It was a frightening experience going into that unit through two sets of locks and wondering what would be taking place behind those big doors. I reported to three "specialists," who were there in a heartbeat to meet me—almost as if my being there was going to be a really special part of their day. Immediately, I was told that I would be meeting with one of the patients from the unit to conduct my preliminary assessment of the difficulties he was having. I was also told that my interactions with this patient would be observed from behind a one-way glass and that I would get feedback on how well I did. This all seemed very important. I sat down at a gray desk in a sterile little office with a really high ceiling awaiting my first human service experience.

Moments later, the specialists were back: one on each side of the patient, holding the patient's arms at his sides, and one

5

bringing up the rear. They physically guided him into a vinyl and chrome chair facing me and instructed him in no uncertain terms to stay seated. Frightened as I probably appeared, I'm surprised they didn't tell me the same thing! They left the room for the observation area.

Although my vision of this young man has been tainted by time, I recall that I was moved by his light blue hospital gown, his unkempt appearance, his smell, and his extremely distant, unfocused gaze. He was just a kid, very much like me. There I was, getting ready to help. I noticed that some of my fear started to subside.

Knowing that part of my mission was to gather information, I started with a simple greeting, "Hi, my name is Marty. What's yours?" There was no response: no words, no movement, not even a glance in my direction. Thinking that maybe he hadn't heard me or that maybe I was so nervous I didn't actually greet him out loud, I repeated a little louder, "Hi, my name is Marty. What's yours?" Again, there was only silence. I decided to mix it up a little bit. I said something like, "I'm from Illinois. Where are you from?" No response. "I really like music. Who's your favorite band?" No response. This one-way conversation continued for some time.

Finally, the silence was broken in a way that I have never been able to forget. The sound was not part of a breakthrough from my efforts to verbally communicate with this young kid. It was the unmistakable sound of the specialists who were observing us from behind the one-way glass attempting to control their laughter. It got louder and louder and louder until finally they reentered the room, red-faced, and escorted the patient away in the same manner they had brought him. They never returned to the office to give me feedback on how well I did. I sat there for a really long time and finally just left for the rest of the afternoon.

That evening back at the barracks, I continued to think about my first human service experience. Was this the way that people interacted in a helping situation? I talked to a few of my friends about what had happened and used a little of their help to get over it. I did my own little diagnosis, decided that he probably was not deaf, and concluded that this young man was probably experiencing something called *catatonic schizophrenia*. This major psychosis can be characterized by total withdrawal, lack of communication, extreme apathy, and so on. Because the military training manual didn't say much about how catatonia was treated, I figured I would just go back the next day and try out some different things. I certainly didn't know any better. Maybe instead of talking, we would go for a walk together. Maybe we would get out of that dull unit and into the sunshine. Maybe I could just get him to look at me. Maybe.

I returned through the secured doors the next afternoon, nervous again yet ready to go. I saw the specialists, but I walked by them to the nurses' station. I asked where I could find the patient. There was some hesitation and brief eye contact between the nurses and the specialists. I asked again. Finally, I was informed that he was no longer on the unit. He had been transferred to medical intensive care. He had stabbed himself with an ice pick that morning during a crafts group. I was deeply moved by this information. I walked around the unit in my own sort of daze, interacting with anyone who looked like a patient and doing my very best to avoid having to communicate with the specialists. I was more frightened by the possibility of talking with them than anything the patients were doing.

I suppose I thought about things in a behavioral way before I learned anything about behaviorism. As long as I can remember, I was always interested in *why* things occurred and I always believed there were reasons for what happens.[1] From this experience, I concluded that the patient stabbed himself as a result of something in the *interaction* that had taken place the previous afternoon. I was absolutely convinced that somehow he must have heard the laughter, saw the red faces, and felt extreme sorrow, pain, or helplessness that led to his intense emotional response. I don't know whether this conclusion is accurate, but I believe it to this day. The whole experience has had an important impact on the way I approach helping others. In a loosely behavioral way, it has become one of the reasons or causes for some of the things I say and do.

Of course, this particular military experience was not the last time I witnessed people in helping roles interact in ways that probably caused more harm than good; however, the experience seems to have enhanced my sensitivity to the profound impact such interactions may have. *Helping others is fundamentally about interacting in a way that produces some sort of desired change for the person being helped.* If you interact in a way that directly or indirectly produces harm, then you are not helping.

Yet, it is remarkable how often these sorts of harmful interactions take place in human service situations. Sometimes, such an interaction is obvious. If a potential helper makes a blatantly rude comment and a person in need of assistance immediately walks away, we can be reasonably sure that no helping has taken place. Individuals within human service situations may also insult, correct, instruct, lecture, direct, give stern looks to, coerce, reprimand, scold, make fun of, hurt, laugh at, force, or otherwise abuse people in ways that regularly produce this effect. Some may even believe that these ways of interacting are exactly what people need in order to "get better." If you should meet or interact with one of these people, consider being at least skeptical and perhaps appalled, particularly if you notice that no one is coming to them for help. In general, be very alert to any sort of interaction that may reduce the likelihood that a person in need of assistance will demonstrate a desire to interact with you or other potential helpers. It is hard to help a person who has no interest in being with you.

---

[1]A few years later, I learned that there was a philosophy (behaviorism), a science (the experimental analysis of behavior), and a technology (behavior analysis and therapy) that dealt with the relationships between life situations and behavior, and I began to read books by Skinner (1971), Kazdin (1975), and others who greatly influenced the way I thought and the way I attempted to help.

Interactions that drive an individual away are easily spotted, but other potentially harmful interactions are not quite so obvious. The second type of interaction that usually has little chance of helping is failing to respond when a person in need of assistance seeks out interaction. All of us have had this sort of experience. You know that a person is seeking you out, but you do nothing to encourage an interaction. Yet, if an individual who needs help does not seek out interaction, you cannot be in a position to provide any help and the individual cannot be in a position to get any. The clearest and most frequent way that this sort of interaction occurs in human service situations is when helpers ignore requests for interaction.

There are lots of potential problems with the interactional strategy that people casually refer to as *ignoring*, not the least of which is that it sometimes works and people in need of assistance stop seeking interaction. If people in need of assistance stop seeking help, things are not likely to get better and instead are likely to get worse. As a result of being ignored, some people who are considered to be disabled have stopped seeking the assistance that they might be able to use to enhance their lives.

The third type of interaction that might have some chance of helping but often winds up being harmful is when potential helpers make up rules about how an individual is supposed to seek out or request interactions with them. You are likely to hear statements such as, "Sally is just acting like that so she can get your attention." I no longer interpret this sort of statement as bad news. Instead, I try to be pleased that Sally has an interest in my attention, and I look forward to interacting with her so that maybe she can learn a little more about some of the best ways to attain it. I won't discourage her attention seeking by establishing an arbitrary rule, especially if this is my first meeting with Sally or if I suspect she would have great difficulty learning such a rule. If she seeks attention in troublesome ways, I can worry about that later. First, I need to get to know or learn more about her. People do that by getting an interactional exchange going, not by creating rules that discourage any exchange.

It could be because many people in need of assistance have had such a difficult time establishing interactions with others that they have developed many of their most troublesome ways of requesting attention in the first place. Although learning such skills may be very important at some point in some lives, the message here is that it should not be your primary interest when you are in the process of establishing a potential helping relationship. You need to get yourself in a position to help, and you do that by interacting in particular ways that I discuss in later objectives.

Although we may do our best to do no harm, it is important to recognize that some others with whom we interact in helping situations may not use the same styles. In fact, you may meet individuals who will criticize your use of these styles and directly or indirectly encourage you to use different ones. This is a remarkable thing, particularly when it is done by an individual who has spent a long time in a situation where they might have been a helper. It may be useful, as you are getting ready to help, to be alert for some of these other styles because they may negatively affect people's lives. It could be that some of these ways of interacting are potentially responsible for some of the very problems you may wish to address (e.g., when individuals learn to get a helper's attention by behaving in a dangerous way).

Thinking about others you have watched or heard who were in a situation in which they might have been able to help but didn't (e.g., store clerks, receptionists, co-workers) can help you recognize negative interactional styles. You may also recognize them from time to time in your own behavior. I know that I have noticed them in mine. Some of these interactional styles may be characterized as follows:

- Go away. Don't bother me.
- I have the answers, but people just don't listen.
- These people have [whatever diagnosis or problem]. They won't change.
- People like this just need to be told what to do.
- Nothing is going to change for [the person who needs help]. He is just that way.

- These people are beyond hope.
- I just do this kind of work because I have to.
- You think you have problems? Let me tell you how good you have it.
- What I know is way beyond your intellectual capacity.
- I haven't noticed one good thing about you.
- Don't expect to get anything done under these conditions.
- It'll never work. We tried that already.
- We're not here to be their friends.
- If this was supposed to be any fun, they wouldn't have to pay you for doing it.
- I'm too deep in thought to be concerned with that.
- I have too many other things going on in my life to get involved.
- My paperwork is more important than you are.
- I don't have a clue how to help you.

SUMMARY

Increasing your sensitivity or ability to observe the effects of your own behavior on an individual's interest in interacting with you is a vital part of getting ready to help. Be alert to several types of negative interaction that occur in human service situations so that you can avoid them and increase your chances of being viewed as a good helper by those you are attempting to help. Three general ways may hurt your chances of getting in a position to help and may also produce harm to others:

1. Having interactions that drive others away from you
2. Failing to respond when others first seek out interactions with you
3. Making up rules about what is expected in order to have an interaction with you in the first place

I never found out what happened to the young man who stabbed himself. It is strange that I don't even remember going back to that place again. I was transferred almost right after it all happened. I hope he found someone who could help him or that someone who could help found him. As hard a lesson as it was, I learned something very important from those specialists. It appears to be true in all sorts of helping relationships. First, do no harm.

Don't Blame

I spent 9 years working exclusively with people who had experienced brain injuries as a result of traumatic events like car or train accidents, falls, gunshot wounds, assaults, and so on. I know I had met many people who had brain injuries earlier in my life, but they were often called "mentally ill," "developmentally disabled," or some other thing. I have noticed that good helpers usually try to call people by their names, rather than by some description that has been made up for their disability or illness.

Acquired brain injury is an amazing thing. A life can seem to be headed one way, and in a few brief moments, literally everything can change. A person's ability to move, speak, see, hear, think, feel, engage in personal care, have relationships, work, and much more can be changed in an instant. A person may not even remember what life was like without the injury. According to any definition of acquired brain injury, these changes occur as a result of neurological or physical insults to the brain (as opposed to a change in some personality characteristic, personal habit, or religious belief). In other words, it would seem as though such changes might be *expected* as a result of neurological damage to particular parts of the brain. Yet, this is not the impression I have gotten many times when I have watched potential helpers interact with people who experienced brain injuries.

The issue of what to expect has become important to me because of the number of times I have witnessed a family member, friend, loved one, or even a rehabilitation professional expect things to be different than they are for an individual and then become frustrated when things don't change. This pattern often becomes more evident as time passes following the injury and an individual fails to progress as expected. Don't be mistaken. Having expectations for change is generally a great thing, and many believe that expecting change is critical to producing change. Sometimes, I think that way. However, expectations that lead to frustration can become problematic when they affect how potential helpers interact with the people they are attempting to help. This problem seems to develop frequently when potential helpers become frustrated with how an individual acts or behaves and then begin to treat that person differently.

I have never heard a helper angrily raise his or her voice to an individual who was physically unable to walk independently in order to try to prompt that person to walk. In most of these situations, we recognize that walking probably will not occur, and we adjust our expectations and actions accordingly. Partially as a result, some helpers have done an incredible job of creating equipment that permits many people who cannot walk independently to get around. Furthermore, many adjustments have been made to communities in order to make them more accessible to these individuals (e.g., sidewalk modifications, ramps, lifts for vehicles). Laws have been passed to protect individuals' rights to inclusion in society. People seem to understand when current helping abilities and technology are not likely to produce changes in walking for some individuals, and adjustments are made to accommodate each individual's difficulty and to meet his or her needs more easily. It wasn't always this way for people who could not ambulate independently. Partially as a result of adjusting expectations, some very exciting changes have occurred in many communities.

What concerns me, however, is that it still seems like society's attitudes, expectations, and actions have not evolved concerning expectations for people who *behave* differently. I see people expecting, instructing, and even cajoling these individuals to change their behavior all of the time. For example, I once knew a man who was so incredibly confused following a severe frontal lobe brain injury that he often could not recall his own name, spoke to plants as if they were people, and interpreted blindness in his left eye as "a little difficulty" with his sight. Yet, I noticed that some people who were supposed to assist him would become frustrated with him when he failed to respond to what they viewed as simple requests (e.g., to take his dishes into the kitchen and put them in the sink). It was as if they expected to "fix" his brain injury by simply instructing him to behave differently. Many of these helpers became frustrated with his lack of response to their instructions and began to refer to his behavior as noncompliant. As a result of their faulty expectations, they began to interact differently with him and to voice their disappointment in his lack of progress. Initially, it was very difficult to encourage them to view things differently.

This sort of problem can become apparent within helping relationships, as well as in everyday interactions with others. For example, it often seems okay if the person who behaves differently is not invited to a gathering, excused from the restaurant, separated from the group, kept away from children, or kicked out of town. We know this. It is all around us. It has been taking place for centuries. Although situations may exist in which these sorts of actions seem justifiable, we benefit from continuing to increase our willingness to include people.

So, why is it that helpers sometimes *interact* differently when it comes to people who behave differently? One of the most influential behaviorists of our time had some interesting thoughts that relate to this matter. B.F. Skinner wrote in *Beyond Freedom and Dignity* that "There may be a natural inclination to be reinforcing to those who reinforce us, as there is to attack those who attack us . . . " (1971, p. 42). In other words, we may have an automatic tendency to be good to those people who are good to us and to treat poorly those people whom we view as treating us poorly. Skinner's statement (and my paraphrase of it) has become one of the most powerful, guiding tenets not only of my human service career but also of my entire life. I notice its truth all the time in my own actions and the actions of those around me. I see it at meetings, in stores, at sports events, in other people's words, and on the nightly news. I see it in my own actions when I am kind or return a favor to someone who has been kind or has done a favor for me and when I am regularly tempted to be rude to someone who has been rude to me. It can seem so incredibly encompassing, compelling, and obvious.

A number of things can be learned from more closely examining Skinner's statement. To me, one of the most important of these has to do with the words *natural inclination*. What is a natural inclination? Put simply, a behaviorist might describe a natural inclination as a predictable or reasonable result of everything that has come before: a person's heritage, genetic makeup, learning history, experience, and whole life up to now. It represents how someone might be expected to act based on everything that has happened before. So, with respect to interacting with others, it appears that Skinner has suggested that it is *natural* to treat some people one way and other people another way based on our history so far of interacting with other people. If you are *reinforcing* with some people (i.e., behaving in a way that increases the probability of future interactions with them), you shouldn't be surprised. It is a natural inclination and probably the result of being treated in that way by them or somebody else like them in your past. If you attack some other people, you also shouldn't be surprised. It is a natural result of being treated that way by them or somebody else like them in your past.

But taking the notion of natural inclination a bit farther begins to reveal something potentially very important and extremely useful in this behaviorist view of the world: natural results, predictability, relationships between things, no real surprises. Predictability is one of the hallmarks of science. In all of nature, things are caused, including the ways that every person behaves. If you observe closely, you begin to see causes all around you. You see them in the things you do and the things that others do. People behave in certain ways for reasons. I was happy yesterday because I got good news about something I wanted.

I am irritable today because I didn't sleep well last night. I am feeling foggy headed because I took cold medicine 2 hours ago. I am writing this book because there are things I wish to communicate and others have encouraged me to write it. I wear reading glasses because I see better with them. John has things written out for him because he has had a neurological insult to his brain and, as a result, cannot understand or process spoken words. *Things happen because of all of the other things that have happened before.* We don't always know what they were, and we usually don't even try to find out. Most of the time in our own lives, discovering the cause doesn't matter. We just know that things happen for a reason, and all of the reasons have come before.

The point here is to instill a deeper appreciation of the idea that people do the things they do in their lives for a reason or some combination of reasons, some that another person can figure out and others that probably won't be discovered. Figuring out all of the reasons for the things people do is not the most important part, although some people are primarily interested in that. It is more important to allow yourself to see that if the things that people do are caused (by this or that or the other thing that has gone before), then you are probably being unreasonable when you become frustrated and hold people to blame for the things that they think, feel, and do. It may be enough for you to know that they think, feel, and do all of those things for good reasons.

This way of thinking about people's actions is at the root of interacting from a position of no blame in your helping relationships with others. Put simply, a position of no blame proposes that if people behave in certain ways as a result of all of the things that have come before, then holding them at fault or to blame for their actions does not make good sense. If frustration arises, it might be more reasonably directed toward the causes of the behavior, as opposed to the individual. This does not mean that people should be encouraged to behave any way they like and that you just have to be okay with that. We can usually count on social guidelines (customs, rules, and laws) to help ensure that people will be held accountable for the things that they do, whether it changes their future behavior or not. However, it does mean that, as someone who is interested in helping, you should be especially sensitive to the notion that people do the things that they do for a reason, and you should attempt to refrain from blaming them personally for these things.

Increasing your sensitivity to the *reasons* that people do things, as well as the actual things that they do, can change the way you approach a helping situation and the way you interact once you are in it.

- Acquired brain injury causes changes to the brain that make particular sorts of behavior more or less likely than before. Knowing that, you can carry a deeper sense of the whole picture when you are making decisions about how someone will be treated.

- Being physically abused as a child may account for many unusual but understandable things a person does as an adult. You can increase your own sensitivity to the amazing things that happen to people and not be so surprised by the way that they may respond to them.

- Growing up with a learning difficulty is not easy. You can begin to be a little more understanding and perhaps forgiving when you consider that, had those kinds of things happened to you, you might be responding in some of the same unusual or unwanted ways.

By cautiously reconsidering some of these philosophical behavioral perspectives, helpers can begin to treat people without blaming them for the things that they do. You will have begun to overcome the natural inclination to treat people as you always have. You will change. As a result, the people receiving help will see a difference in their helper. Others will see it in your actions, and they will have more interest in interacting with you because you are not constantly blaming them for the "mistakes" they may make.

Making this change is very important because it can produce a very powerful experience of acceptance of others, of different ways of doing things, of diversity in the world. It is also important because when people fall into the blaming trap, they may begin to treat others less humanely. Problem behavior becomes more than just the result of things that have come before. Inadvertently, people begin to hold the individual at fault for behavior that they don't like. It becomes the individual's fault that he behaved as he did, that she said what she said, that he is the way he is. Finding fault is likely to make you much less effective in your interactions with people whom you may wish to help. It provides a reason to begin acting with less dignity and respect toward the individual receiving help. After all, if the unwanted behavior is an individual's fault, then it seems okay for potential helpers to treat that person any way they choose, including roughly or rudely.

It is rare to hear blaming taking place without seeing it followed by some sort of negative action from potential helpers. Watch for these things and you will see that inaccurate thinking about what causes behavior often leads to blaming people for the things they do. Blaming people leads to fault finding. Fault finding leads to treating people rudely. Treating people rudely almost never changes their behavior in a desired way. It usually leads to more rude behavior.

SUMMARY

So far, I have presented two very important ideas that may guide you as you get ready to help. First, do no harm. Don't drive people in need of assistance away from you, don't ignore their requests for interaction, and don't demand that they make their requests for help in a particular way that is not yet possible or interesting to them. Second, don't blame people for the things that they do. If you notice that you are upset with someone you are attempting to help or that you are about to treat them rudely, you can be fairly sure you have gotten stuck in a blame trap. Try to get around your natural inclination. Remind yourself that people do the things they do for a reason. Look for the causes or the reasons for the things that they do. If you can't find them, just trust that they are there. If you can avoid doing harm and blaming, you are likely to become a better helper. In addition, you may be less frustrated or upset by some of the troubling situations that occur when people need help. People in need of help will be more likely to want to be around you, and even those who don't need your help will know that there is something different and perhaps even special about you. You will have begun to overcome some of your natural inclinations. Helping may begin to feel even better.

Watch for Reciprocity

We are naturally inclined to be reinforcing to those who reinforce us and to attack those who attack us. This statement often entails two very different ways of interacting with other people. Nate Azrin, a very creative man, was moved by this idea and began to study some of the ways that people relate to each other. It is reasonable that he would become interested in this idea in part because he was a student of B.F. Skinner at Harvard.

Azrin began to use the term *reciprocity* to describe these types of relationships. (Although Azrin studied various forms of cooperative behavior in the late 1960s, he began using the term *reciprocity* in the context of marital counseling and other learning-based therapies a decade later in 1978.) Expressed most simply, *reciprocity* is an ongoing exchange of similar interactions between people. The two clearest types of reciprocal relationships are 1) reinforce–reinforce and 2) attack–attack. Of course, these are the two extremes. For example, attack–attack interactions do not just refer to those exchanges that involve physical aggression. People have many more ongoing interactions with others that don't include actual aggression but may be characterized as attacks because the interactions are displeasing, unwanted, distasteful, critical, discounting, or otherwise unpleasant. People are likely to have many more of this kind of attack relationship with others than they are to actually engage in ongoing physical aggression. Someone criticizes you, and you find yourself criticizing back. A soccer player trips a competitor on the field, and the crowd cheers when he or she is treated roughly in return. A person violates a member of our family or our culture, and we vote for leaders who are likely to support some form of revenge.

An ongoing reinforce–reinforce reciprocal interaction can also be called a *mutually reinforcing relationship.* Creating this sort of interaction is an extremely important objective as you are getting ready to help. The range of exchanges that fall in the reinforce–reinforce category is also very broad. People may have ongoing exchanges of reinforce–reinforce interactions with different individuals that look and sound very different. Good examples include exchanges of eye contact or comments between individuals who are flirting, complementary solo performances in a bluegrass band, a regular exchange of acknowledgments between particular co-workers, and public-supported employer compensation benefits for hiring workers diagnosed with disabilities.

The key in any type of reciprocal relationship is the ongoing nature of the interactional exchange between the individuals involved. A reciprocal exchange of interactions may take place between two or more individuals, groups of individuals (e.g., two teams who have developed a longstanding rivalry), neighbors (e.g., the Hatfields and the McCoys), governments, cultures, or even countries (e.g., the United States and Cuba). This book focuses on how two individuals relate to each other because most of you will find yourselves in this kind of helping relationship.

To establish a potentially helpful interaction, one of the people involved has to initiate, or start, the process. People don't usually think too much about how interactional processes get started, but it may be very important. For example, in 1997, I had the opportunity to visit a rehabilitation hospital to evaluate a person for admission to a community-based treatment program I was directing. When I first arrived on the unit, the staff told me that

I should expect to be verbally and physically attacked when I met the young woman and that I should be very careful to protect myself if she threw things or got too close to me. Of course, many people would have no interest in walking into a situation in which they knew they were likely to be attacked. In fact, it seems pretty natural that most would probably want to go in the opposite direction. When people anticipate being attacked, they usually look for something else to do. This is a predictable and reasonable response that could even be expected based on people's natural inclinations.

However, if you wish to get yourself in a position to help, you will have to overcome your natural inclination or desire to walk away because people very rarely do better by themselves. Social isolation is often likely to make things worse. So, after lightly tapping on the door, I entered the young woman's room. In this situation, the staff were absolutely right. She immediately sat up on her bed and began screaming very loudly a clear stream of profanities about my ancestry, her fighting skills, and her desire to hurt me. She threw a hairbrush and a small picture frame that were next to her on the nightstand. As I ducked slightly, they cruised over my head and hit the wall behind me.

Before we consider what to do in a situation like this (see Objective Six), we must ask ourselves why someone would act like this in the presence of someone he or she had never met. She and I had no previous history of interaction. Why would someone whom I had never met immediately attack when given her first opportunity? I reminded myself that people do things for a reason. She must have reasons. Maybe if I could understand the reasons, I could understand why this was happening and keep myself from becoming upset, frustrated, or hurtful. I began to use my experience. I also reminded myself not to blame her for the things that she was doing. I just assumed that *she* was not to blame.

Several reasons became very apparent when I had a chance to learn more about her from her hospital records. About a year earlier, she had experienced a very severe injury to the frontal lobe of her brain. I knew that among many other things, the frontal lobe helps keep people from saying or doing all of the silly or strange things everyone thinks about saying or doing. She had received very little, if any, help to relearn how to manage her impulses after the injury. In fact, she had spent almost all of the past year of her life being physically cared for in a remote nursing home. She had been mechanically restrained to her bed on a near daily basis during that year. I knew that she had no idea what had happened to her, where she was, or who all of these people were around her. She was only able to state her name correctly about two of every ten times she was asked. To her, I was just another caregiver. Of course she would attack me. It made almost perfect sense. There were plenty of good reasons for her to attack me.

I tried to imagine being so confused but unable to do things any differently. I tried to imagine having such a serious injury in a huge medical complex with so many different people coming and going. I tried to imagine some of the silly or strange things I might say and do if I experienced a frontal lobe brain injury. I tried to imagine what it would be like to be uncertain about my own name and have others take physical hold of me (for what?) and mechanically tie me to a bed or a wheelchair. I tried to imagine what extra, added fear this might produce for me if I were a woman. I tried to imagine how she would possibly make sense out of any of these things. I tried to imagine her history of being treated by others, and I reached the conclusion that she had lots of very good reasons to attack me. Maybe I would go away.

If you are going to get yourself in a position to help, you cannot attack back, you cannot ignore, and you cannot go away when the situation gets difficult. I didn't always understand these things, and even when I began to understand them, I didn't always act in a way that was likely to help. I hope you won't hold me to blame for this. At the time, I was just doing what I was naturally inclined, and sometimes even encouraged, to do.

There is a fairly easy way to understand what may be going on when you confront these kinds of situations or as you are attempting to be able to help someone else. I have come to think of it as the *heat.* Behavioral research suggests that, when life becomes difficult or the heat comes on, a person responds in one of only four general ways: 1) attempt to get away from the heat, 2) freeze or withdraw in the midst of the heat, 3) become emotional, or 4) act in ways that are specifically designed to make the heat go away. (I am extrapolating here from research on escape and avoidance, conditioned emotional responding, and problem-solving behavior, as opposed to a single study that would support my conclusion.) Observation has helped me learn that

- What causes difficulty or heat may be different for different people
- An individual who is in the midst of a difficult situation may act in one or more of the four ways
- These ways do not necessarily occur in any particular order
- An individual is often more likely to respond in his or her *characteristic* way on a regular basis than he or she is to respond differently each time

In other words, some people always seem to try escaping or avoiding tough situations in life, others generally withdraw when the going gets difficult, and many others seem to get emotional all the time. Then, there are those other people who rarely seem to use any of those three ways and go directly to acting in ways that are designed to make the heat go away. These are remarkable people. Find them and be around them.

In my personal and human service experience, I have noticed that looking for what causes the heat and observing how people respond to it in these ways has helped a great deal. For example, I have noticed that when *I* am either avoiding something, frozen in inaction, or clearly emotional, it is a sign that the heat is on in some way in my life. For me, noticing these things is now a signal to look for the causes and get ready for action.

It also seems that if a particular way of reacting to the heat is not available for an individual, one or more of the other ways are more likely to show up. For the young woman at the hospital, two ways of responding to the heat were just not available to her. She would have a very hard time getting away from the heat because she could not ambulate independently, and her ability to act in ways that were specifically designed to reduce the heat was seriously limited by her brain injury. Therefore, either withdrawing in the midst of the heat or responding in a very intensely emotional way were much more likely reactions for her.

In general, the first three ways of responding to the heat (getting away from it, withdrawing, and getting emotional) don't work very consistently as ways to actually reduce the heat, and sometimes these ways can make a bad situation worse (e.g., when getting emotional produces danger in one's own life or the lives of others). It appears that really only one way of responding works very effectively to handle the difficult situations that pro-duce heat—learning how to act in ways that are designed to make the heat go away. We have all learned a few of these ways. I have tried to learn *not* to respond in ways that are the *least* likely to help reduce the heat. As a result, I don't notice myself avoiding tough situations as often or becoming as emotional, at least to the degree that it presents major difficulties in my life. If you think about it, you may notice the same things in your life, and this is probably a factor in some of your successes to date.

One year after her severe acquired brain injury and in the midst of the heat that my presence was creating for her, the young woman at the hospital really seemed to have no choice but to respond emotionally. I felt that I understood her. I believed that she had good reasons. I didn't take it personally because it simply wasn't personal. Even in circumstances like this, a huge part of your mission as a helper is to establish a different type of reciprocal relationship, not one that is based on attack–attack but one that is based on establishing an ongoing exchange of positively reinforcing interactions. *Helpers cannot count on the person in need of assistance to start a mutually reinforcing interaction.* Most of the time, unless someone has clearly come to you for help, you are going to have to start the process. This is the basis of a helper's role, and you will see that it can become a remarkably exciting role to have.

SUMMARY

As you begin to observe, understand, and experience reciprocity in all of your human interactions, you can see many examples of ongoing attack–attack and reinforce–reinforce relationships that seem to go on and on between individuals, groups, governments, and cultures. Some of the reasons for this are found in the ways that difficult situations can produce heat in people's lives, and the ways they are likely to respond when the heat comes on for them. This isn't surprising when you consider all of the reasons that people may do the things that they do. Each person (including you and me) is probably just doing the best he or she can with whatever experiences are available to draw on. Attacking back when someone attacks you is not only unlikely to get you in a position to help, it is likely to help keep an attack–attack reciprocal interaction going. Your interactions have to be the start of something different.

Create a Mutually Reinforcing Relationship

By now, perhaps you have started to think about some important things in ways that may be very different for you. Some of the ways people act may seem a little more reasonable than before. Perhaps thinking about these things will influence how you deal with yourself and others, especially when you find yourself in a position where help might be provided. You also know several things not to do if you are interested in helping.

The next objective as you get ready to help is to establish, as rapidly as possible, a mutually reinforcing relationship with the person you are attempting to assist. Unfortunately, no one can really learn exactly how to do this from reading about it in a book. You learn about it through considering your interactional experience to date, practicing new ways of interacting in a variety of different helping situations, and seeing or hearing about the effects of your interactions. You also learn by being encouraged to build mutually reinforcing relationships and being acknowledged for doing so by others (see Objective Eight).

Think about a great relationship you have had in your life: with a sister, brother, parent, co-worker, classmate, friend, lover, anyone. Maybe the relationship lasted for years or maybe just a day or even just a few hours. After you have someone in mind, think about a special time that you shared, a time when you felt very happy, fulfilled, joyful, glad, or however you describe the feeling you most enjoyed and desired. Now ask yourself, what was it about that person and that time that was so special? Why did you feel so good? Do you think the other person felt some of the same great things you felt? Try to take your time with this exercise and hold onto whatever thoughts you are having as you continue reading.

As I think back on some of my human service memories, one of the neatest relationships I can recall was with another young woman I will call Lilly. Lilly was one of the most special people I have ever met. I met Lilly while working as a research assistant at a very fine laboratory that was based at a large mental health and developmental center that still exists about 8 miles from my home. Lilly had lived at this center for years on the same large unit with many people who had also lived or worked there for years. From all indications, Lilly could speak only two words (her first and last names), and she would not do this very often unless, as staff reported, she was in a particularly happy mood. According to the reports in her record, Lilly was considered to have a pervasive developmental disability, no testable IQ, and virtually no adaptive skills whatsoever. Everybody else who lived on this unit was reported to be in the same condition, although they were all very different people.

My job was to bring Lilly back and forth to the research laboratory several times per day so that the research team could use her help to learn more about *stereotypy*, or, as others called it, self-stimulation. If Lilly was dressed in pants with a zipper, she would spend most of her waking moments raising and lowering the zipper up and down, faster, slower, up and down again and again. This behavior was very interesting to the research team, and the team was looking for ways to explain *why* it occurred and how it might be changed. At the time, I never thought very much about why anyone thought it *should* be changed, but I guess zipping could have distracted her from other potentially productive activities or could have attracted critical attention if she were to live somewhere other than at a state mental health and developmental center.

Lilly and I spent a lot of time together going back and forth from her unit to the lab, from the lab to her unit, faster, slower, again and again. In the early going, I didn't think about our interactions very much. In fact, I am not even sure I considered that we were actually having any interaction because we didn't talk. I would just go to the unit, find her among the crowd, make sure she was dry and dressed in pants with a zipper, take her by the hand, and escort her silently up and down the steps and through the halls from the unit to the testing room and back. This was my job, and most days it just seemed like a chore.

I'm really not sure who started it, but one day I noticed that Lilly and I had begun interacting with each other in a new way. With eye contact, subtle facial expressions, sounds, and touch, we began to establish a characteristic interactional pattern. She would spot me on the unit, and we would make eye contact. I would smile, and she would smile (or not). I would say "Lilly" in a high pitch just like she said it, and she would say "Lilly" (or not). I would move toward the big door. She would move toward the big door and wait. I would unlock the door and say, "Let's walk the steps." She always would. I would tap the back of her calf if she used the "two feet per step" method rather than the "one foot per step" method (which was much quicker and looked more typical), and we would often find tons of little things to smile and sometimes laugh out loud about as we went. Sometimes, though, we wouldn't. Sometimes, we would just go along in silence, making very occasional eye contact. Those quiet days were great, too. It made me wonder what had happened to create such seriousness. Sometimes, we would even share some vanilla ice cream after the hard work of the testing sessions.

I'm honestly not sure which of us found this interaction more reinforcing, interesting, and fun, but it was clearly all of those things. I also noticed that not only was it fun and mutually enjoyable, we *both* were learning things as a result of interacting. Lilly learned how to walk steps really well. She learned how to hold her own spoon when we had ice cream. She learned how to change out of wet pants if dry pants were laid out and I asked her to "go change pants?" She smiled a lot more often than she had before.

I learned that it was very possible to communicate pretty fully with a person who did not use words. There are all sorts of ways to teach people new things as you go about the process of interacting with each other, rather than always setting up artificial situations to teach particular skills (see Objective Seven). I learned that teaching could be really fun instead of a chore for potential learners and teachers. I learned that it was possible to have a mutually reinforcing friendship with a person who was considered to have a pervasive developmental disability and an untestable IQ. I learned these things the first time that Lilly walked toward me on her own, took my hand, and smiled without my prompts.

A mutually reinforcing relationship (e.g., one that is based on an ongoing exchange of pleasant, desired, useful, or otherwise beneficial interactions) is not an easy thing to describe. About the time you think you have a good description nailed, someone will be likely to argue that it wasn't that way for them or that you are somehow mistaken. So, I won't try here to describe what it is like. I suggest instead that we have all had bits and pieces of this sort of a relationship, if not a full blown and lasting experience of the excitement, joy, and potential for learning that it can produce. I also suggest that most of us recognize when it is taking or has taken place for us (think back to the memory I prompted you to recall and hold a moment ago). It is in the memory of a special person or a special time. It is in my memories of Lilly. It just feels good, and, in general, most of us would like to have more of this feeling in our lives.

What does it take for people to be able to have and share this sort of experience more often in their personal lives and in potential helping relationships? There are some practices you can follow that will likely allow you to experience it more often and, as a result, possibly become a better helper. Getting ready to help is about considering these things, putting them into practice, looking for the results, and going back for more.

When you initiate or try to set yourself up in a position to help, you need to remember that your objective is to establish a mutually reinforcing relationship that *both* individuals are interested in having. It is unlikely that you will be in a position to help if you don't have or pursue this kind of relationship. Resist your inclination to treat people poorly or blame them for things they are currently saying or doing. Helpers cannot avoid the problem if they want to help. They have to get closer to it.

How can you teach yourself to do these things? Perhaps as important as anything else, as Lovett (1996) highlighted so clearly, you need to learn to listen very closely to the individual you are attempting to help. Although helping *is* to a certain degree about your interests (e.g., to experience the great feeling of having a mutually reinforcing relationship), you need to put your interests aside in the early stages of a relationship so that the person you wish to help can communicate with you as fully as possible in whatever ways he or she can. Remember, this person probably won't communicate on your terms, with your expressions and your words. Individuals usually communicate in ways they have learned from their experiences. In order to establish a mutually reinforcing relationship, you need to *listen with all of your senses.*

Among many other things, listening with all of your senses means being very sensitive to the words or sounds that people make, their expressions and movement, and their response to and desire for contact with you. It means successfully observing the ways that people act, the things that they say and don't say, what they approach, and what they draw away from. It means learning to understand the communicative intent of the things that people do or say and not just the face value of their words or actions. It means paying very close attention to their character-istic interactional styles and watching how these styles change in different situations. Listening with all of your senses means discovering what you can do to encourage a person to approach you in order to establish interaction. Keep reminding yourself that the individual must approach if you are to get in a position to help. You have to learn to listen in a way that others have not.

Once you are confident that an individual is interested in approaching you for help, then you are in a better position to help. It is at this point that the person's responsiveness to your communication, your expectations, and your requests is likely to increase, if only to maintain contact with an important source of reinforcement. However, you have to be cautious that you never stop listening. If you do, you are likely to find out very quickly that you are no longer in a position to help because the person will no longer be interested in approaching you. Helpers cannot be in the best position to help without some sort of contact or interaction. So, a big part of your mission is to interact in ways that are most likely to sustain the reinforcing relationship.

How do helpers interact with all of the different people they want to help in a way that is likely to sustain all of those different relationships? This can seem like a huge task, and it is particularly challenging for people who attempt to provide help in group treatment settings. Another general way to help create mutually reinforcing interactions is to *learn how to communicate in many different ways.* If you are going to become a really good helper, you will need to learn how to communicate effectively as you listen to all of the different individuals whom you attempt to assist. People who need your help cannot be expected to have or to take the time to learn your ways of communicating, your language, your technical terms, or your jargon. You will also have to let the other person know who you are.

Considering the personal way I present the information in this book, it should be clear that I view sharing information about myself, or *self-disclosing,* as a very important part of communicating and developing ongoing relationships with others. Self-disclosure provides information to others as to how they can participate more fully in a mutually reinforcing relationship. This style has been reinforced in many of the most meaningful and productive relationships that I have experienced.

For example, I have had the opportunity to interact with a middle-age man from Serbia for the past several years. This man experienced a very severe brain injury about 12 years ago, just after he came to the United States to find better work for himself and to provide more support to his family back home. After years of rehabilitation in hospitals and small-group residential settings, he now lives in his own apartment in our community. Although his ability to say various English words has always been good, many people have had difficulty understanding that he often does not recall or appreciate the full meaning of many of the words and phrases he uses. In fact, it often appears that he attempts to sound socially correct without recognizing that others don't fully understand what he means (e.g., in a restaurant, he might say, "I like breakfast" when he means either "Please bring me the same thing I ordered yesterday" or "I'd like two fried eggs, one pancake, two pieces of bacon, and coffee"). In order to increase the likelihood of establishing a helping interaction with this man, people providing assistance need to consistently listen, translate, consider the communicative intent of his words, and assist him in communicating more fully (e.g., Carr et al., 1994).

Getting good at listening to this man also means putting his communication in some sort of context, which usually reflects either a particular interest or his cultural background. For example, when he talks incessantly about his need to have more work, it not only suggests that he is probably a little short of money at the time but also that he wishes he could provide more support to his mother in Serbia and overcome his concern about not having a pension that would make him financially secure in his old age. People who understand this context know that when he becomes urgent about his lack of money, it communicates his need to be reminded and reassured about his mother's well-being and his future security as much as anything else. Because of severe memory difficulties following his injury, he often needs this sort of interaction.

His ability to understand spoken English is also very limited due to his experience and his injury. Many people in his community seem to understand this and make adjustments in the way they communicate with him. Those who have taken time to listen and have some interest in ongoing interaction seem to have made some useful adjustments in the way that they communicate. "How you? You want? You feel bad? Come with me? Good coffee?" These people frequently ask if he understands the things they have said to him: "You know? You understand? You like?" It probably sounds pretty funny at times to some who listen, but it works very well for the people trying to communicate. Interaction begins and continues. I have noticed that he seeks out interaction with these people, and they seem to be happy to see him.

During our ongoing relationship, I have attempted to learn some words of his language to let him know that I am interested in communicating with him in a way that we can both understand better. I try not to allow his occasionally angry communications to drive me away or to decrease the frequency of our interactions. As a result, he frequently seeks help from me in his difficult situations, he is usually very receptive to my advice, and he lets me know on a regular basis that I am a "smart man." Of course, I like that.

It may be useful for the sake of contrast to point out that some other people with whom he interacts do not listen so closely and do not attempt to communicate in ways that he understands. Some continue to interact with him as if it is just up to him to somehow communicate more clearly and better understand English, in spite of the fact that his ability to learn these things is seriously limited by his brain injury. I have noticed that, as a result, he rarely seeks out interaction with many of these people and sometimes becomes very frustrated with them.

This example may seem obvious, but many people have had a very difficult time adjusting their communication in a way that has helped him and them. You need to learn many other, more complex ways to communicate. Many methods of communication are nonverbal. We communicate with our eyes, with our facial expressions, with our hand gestures, and with our bodies. If you think about your own interest in being around certain people, you can see that it has a great deal to do with the words that others say to you, as well as the way they *appear* when you meet them.

If you are listening with all of your senses and communicating in many different ways in order to establish and maintain an ongoing interaction, then you are ready to help. Establishing a mutual exchange of potential reinforcers provides the basis for everything that will follow. Without that exchange, you are not in a position to help. In fact, in many situations, you may be in a position to be ignored or attacked. How many times have you avoided or even criticized an individual who you thought had no interest in interacting with you?

After characteristic interaction has been established through listening and communicating in different ways, the process of helping becomes a bit more complex but still very understandable if you focus on maintaining the mutually reinforcing relationship that has been developed. Deeper consideration of the concept of reinforcement may help you in this regard. Simply put (within a context of a helping interaction), a *reinforcer* is anything that you say, do, or give that results in the interaction continuing or becoming more frequent. When the exchange continues or becomes more frequent, you can conclude that your action has been reinforcing. If it does not continue or become more frequent, particularly if either person avoids interaction, then the action cannot be viewed as reinforcing.

Determining whether something that you have said, done, or given has acted as a reinforcer for continued interactions can only be determined after the fact (i.e., by looking at the

relationship between your actions and the likelihood of continued interactions). Unfortunately, the delivery of human service
is unlikely to include a detailed analysis or study of these relationships in most of the settings where help may be provided. That
being the case, it might be useful to refrain from making general
assumptions about how individuals will respond to particular
actions (e.g., everyone likes a good pat on the back) and focus
more on repeating those actions that keep the interaction going
in each individual case.

Just because an interactional pattern continues does not necessarily mean that it is resulting in any help or change for the
person in need of help. However, if you have established a
mutually reinforcing interaction with the individual, then you
are probably in a much better position to provide help. Against
a background of mutual reinforcement, you are more likely to
be able to encourage particular changes in a person's life, and
your advice is much more likely to be communicated, accepted,
and used constructively. People in need of help are not only less
likely to resist your assistance, they will be more likely to act in
ways that help continue the mutually reinforcing interaction
with you! This might be considered sharing in the truest sense.

Think of a scale with a bowl on either side of a balancing
bar. On one side of the scale is everything that has gone before;
all of the person's causes, reasons, and experiences that have
resulted in how things are for the individual are in this bowl.
It is big and heavy. Now, picture the other bowl. This is the one
that contains all of your interactions with the person as you have
attempted to get ready to help by listening, communicating, and
creating your mutually reinforcing relationship. If you expect to
produce some change in the way things have been by tossing
an idea, a piece of advice, a request for action, or some other
intervention in the bowl, then it should be clear that the bowl is
going to have to be pretty full of mutually reinforcing interactions
before changes happen. In my opinion, this is the picture of what
helping is about. In fact, your ability to help may have less to
do with the goodness of the idea, advice, request, or intervention
than it does with the weight of the bowl you have created through

reinforcing interactions with the individual *before* you actually request or encourage any change in behavior. This must be similar to what people mean when they say that a person has to be ready to change or has to want to change.

At the point that you introduce ideas, advice, requests, or interventions into the situation, you need to watch very closely to see what happens. If you are expecting too much too quickly, all sorts of things can occur. The new bowl can tip and all of the things that have gone before can come crashing down more frequently or worse than ever before, leaving you to start over. If you are doing too little too slowly, the weight of everything that has gone before will gradually overpower the reinforcing strength of your interaction. You may continue to have some mutually reinforcing interactions with the individual, but nothing else will change. I don't know if this can really be called helping.

If your ideas, advice, requests, or interventions remain in proportion to the weight of the past and the reinforcing parts of the present, change may occur and the strength of your mutually reinforcing relationship may continue to grow. The individual in need of help will experience more of the reinforcing aspects of interacting with you and have change in his or her life. As a helper, you will get to experience more of the reinforcing aspects of your help. This is the joy of helping (see Objective Eight).

SUMMARY

As you get ready to help, your primary interest should be establishing a mutually reinforcing relationship with the individual you wish to assist. It is within your role to initiate the interaction and to do what is necessary to have it remain ongoing by listening with all of your senses and communicating in the many different ways that may be needed. Only at this point are you ready to help by cautiously adding ideas, advice, requests, or interventions to the situation.

Teach the Person to Fish

Although this book is about getting ready to help, it may also be important to spend some time considering why and how you actually go about the process of helping once you have developed a mutually reinforcing relationship. Failing to do so might be like planning a good route to a vacation spot without having any idea what you are going to do when you get there.

Many seasoned helpers have very different ideas about the purpose and manner of helping. I suppose differences are to be expected because each of them has had his or her own experiences in situations in which help was expected and each of these situations may have included different philosophical guidelines, practices, and rules. Having been involved with several different human service organizations serving many different individuals who were diagnosed with disabilities, I have noticed that just about the time that people are close to agreeing on guidelines, practices, and rules, some new idea comes along that shakes things up again (e.g., custodial care versus active treatment, tough love versus person-centered planning). To me, it is an indication that there is so much to keep learning.

In Objective One, *helping* was described as interacting in a way that produces some sort of desired change in the life of the person being helped. Although this description was good enough for getting started, now it needs to be expanded to consider the purpose and manner of your help.

Although there are a lot of sayings and adages around, sometimes they are powerful enough to catch on, to be repeated, and to actually become reasons why people do some of the things they do. I heard a great saying from my wife (she didn't claim to have made it up): "Give a person a fish and you will feed him for a day. Teach a person to fish and you may feed him for a lifetime." To me, this powerful statement reflects both the purpose and the manner of helping within a mutually reinforcing relationship with another human being. It suggests that in most helping relationships, simply giving something (e.g., an answer, a piece of advice, a thing that would make an individual feel better) is probably not enough. Such things, although nice, only last for that moment, that situation, or that day. They probably do not result in the individual being any more capable of handling his or her difficulties with less help in the future.

In the 1980s, the Health Care Financing Administration (HCFA; now known as the Centers for Medicare & Medicaid Services [CMS]), the primary public agency that pays for providing help to people, created quite a stir in human services when it declared that it would no longer pay for help that was not intended to result in greater individual independence for the person being helped. This decision created a huge shift for many human service providers from caring for people in a custodial way that might promote their dependence on the helper to actively treating or interacting with them in order to help them achieve more autonomy or independence in their lives (see Objective Seven). Although the scope of this mandate seems to have been narrowed somewhat (e.g., more people who are considered to have disabilities are in prisons now than since the 1980s), the primary point is still a good rule that might guide many of your efforts. In my experience, it is also what most people in need of help actually desire. I don't believe I have ever met an individual in need of help who really did not wish to have the skills to handle his or her difficult situations or life more independently. Partially as a result, I have continued to act as though the primary purpose of helping is to better equip and prepare an individual for the difficult situations he or she may face in life.

PERSONAL INTERVENTION

One general manner of helping is through a sort of interactional or participatory problem-solving process that I have referred to as *personal intervention.* (I began using this approach around 1986, used it as the name for a community-based rehabilitation program in 1992, and began to describe it in print in 1994.) This process embodies aspects of D'Zurilla and Goldfried's (1971) psychosocial problem-solving model, Mahoney and Thoresen's (1974) self-control methods, Carr and colleagues' (1994) functional communication strategies, and probably a host of other helping approaches as well.

As discussed previously, the development or emergence of a mutually reinforcing relationship between two individuals probably produces some changes in both lives. In fact, if an interactional pattern continues, it implies the existence of a reinforcing situation that is likely to produce change as the result of influences of each person's actions and reactions on the other person. In a sense, each person's communication becomes part of the reason or cause that things continue to happen as they do. A great advocate for supporting cultural diversity, Condeluci (1991) supported thinking about helping in this way. His concept of interdependence calls for relating as a goal *and* process of helping, particularly with respect to people diagnosed with disabilities.

In a very generic sense, if you see that a difficult or troublesome situation is changing as a result of your continued interaction with an individual, that is a good thing. In fact, it appears to be the basis of many traditional psychotherapies. However, many situations may require you to become more active in the process if you expect to enhance greater individual independence. Remember that this is where the balance comes in. You cannot move too slowly or too quickly without possibly affecting the mutually reinforcing exchange of interactions that must already exist before you take more active steps to help.

More than anything else, personal intervention is a way of thinking about and organizing the way that you provide more formalized help to people who need it. It embodies a purpose of the help (to teach a person to act or intervene more effectively on his or her own behalf) and a manner in which that help may be provided (through an organized plan). It is intended to reflect some of the things that you might do for yourself when you recognize that you are experiencing difficulty and then act in ways that are successful in reducing that heat in your life. It is potentially useful for helpers and for those they attempt to help. It is probably adaptable to just about any helping situation because it encourages people to organize, guide, and plan their thoughts and actions *before* problems arise. It is intended to keep attention focused on the situation at hand and at the same time teach and reinforce a general, yet individualized, strategy for handling life's most difficult challenges.

Personal intervention is 1) an individualized plan for dealing with one's emotions and behavior when difficult situations arise, 2) a contemporary way of teaching behavioral self-management and providing support for people who are learning, and 3) a strategy for people who have a hard time with solving problems when they become emotionally upset. It is a way to fish. It is what I have noticed that I do when I am experiencing difficulty in my life. It is also intended to reflect some of the things you do when you are experiencing difficulty, although you probably have not described your thoughts and actions with those words. Most people already make these efforts in some way with varying degrees of success. If you observe closely, you may begin to see that everybody does the best they can with the personal intervention skills they have.

You may also begin to see that viewing certain things that people do when difficult situations arise as *maladaptive* is not usually very accurate. Instead, it is useful to consider that the challenging, unwanted, or problematic behavior that a person may exhibit when he or she becomes upset probably represents the most effective way he or she has discovered for addressing difficult situations. Although some behaviors may be challenging, unwanted, or problematic, they may also be very adaptive because they often have the desired result for the individual (e.g., to obtain certain outcomes, to reduce discomfort). Sometimes, referring to behaviors as challenging, unwanted, problematic, or maladaptive represents negative judgment on the part of the person describing the behavior (i.e., for whom does the behavior represent a problem?). Behaviors that are described in those ways are most often the simple result of a person experiencing a temporary lapse in his or her characteristic emotional control, decision making, or situational judgment in difficult situations. Because of issues like this, I usually try to refer to these behaviors as *upsets*. We all have them, and we all need a plan for dealing with them.

There are four key parts to creating a personal intervention plan for coping with difficult situations and the upsets they cause:

1. Recognize when an individual is likely to experience difficulty
2. Identify the individual's characteristic sequence of emotional and behavioral responses when the difficulties arise
3. Identify desired actions that are likely to reduce the difficulties
4. Identify the help that is needed when an individual can't or doesn't act effectively on his or her own

Recognize Difficulties

In order to understand this step a little better, think a bit about your own emotions and behavior. Recognizing when you are likely to have difficulty is a vital part of preparing yourself for effective action. When you do this, you are essentially looking for causes, but finding them may take some practice. It is surprising how often a person can fail to observe the impact of life events or situations on his or her own emotional state of being. Frequently, a person can be well into some sort of unwanted emotional or behavioral pattern (e.g., anger, sadness, jealousy, guilt) before realizing that something difficult is confronting him or her. Someone else may need to ask "What's up with you?" or "What happened?" before the person pauses long enough to even consider that he or she is experiencing anything at all. If you are to become better at managing difficult situations in your life, you are going to have to get a little better at recognizing them. You can do this by observing relationships between the difficult situations that arise and the effects that they can have on your emotions and behavior. This is why, in general, emotions can be such great things. Many of the most troublesome ones are clear signs of impending or existing difficulties.

There are two fairly easy ways to recognize more clearly when you are likely to have difficulties. First, consider the conditions under which you are likely to have a bad day. If you look closely, you may see that there are lots of predisposing conditions that can increase the chances that you will have a bad day. For example, many people report that lack of sleep, feeling ill, getting out of a routine, drinking too much the night before, having trouble with a spouse or kids, or anticipating everything they have to do at work can result in having bad days. If you listen with all of your senses to people who cannot or do not communicate in more conventional ways, you can identify the same sorts of conditions in their lives. For example, it appeared that Lilly was likely to have a bad day if someone with whom she lived was aggressive toward her or if she had experienced a seizure in the previous 24 hours. If you look very closely in advance, you should often be able to see when there is a good chance a person will have some difficulties on a particular day. Then, if you recognize that these conditions exist, you can begin to plan accordingly.

A second way of recognizing when you are likely to have difficulties is to identify some specific situations or events that are likely to produce unwanted emotions in your life. Some people refer to these situations or events as *antecedents* or *triggers* because they often happen right before the clearest signs of emotional or behavioral upset become apparent. However, it may be important to avoid getting locked into thinking that these events *always* occur right before a person gets upset. Sometimes this is not the case. An individual's emotional response may be delayed for hours or even days following the key event that actually produced it. And sometimes the expected emotional response won't occur at all after the event. You can learn a lot by studying what is going on when an individual does not respond in the expected way in the presence of events that usually produce an upset. It can lead toward identification of effective problem-solving alternatives that you can encourage or strengthen.

Most people can identify situations or events that make them upset fairly quickly and easily. Receiving criticism, not being acknowledged for doing something they view as good, being late, getting caught doing something not so good, being frightened by any of a million things that can frighten people, being cut off on the highway, listening to certain music, getting bad news, or having a troubling memory are just a few of the difficult situations or events that may cause emotional or behavioral upset for a particular individual. Once again, if you listen closely to the people you are attempting to assist, you can identify the same sorts of things in their lives. You are just learning to observe—looking for relationships between events that happen and people's actions, looking for the causes, looking for what sets up the conditions for difficulty, and looking for the specific events that are likely to start a characteristic sequence of upset.

Identify the Characteristic Sequence

After you have studied the conditions and events that *precede* a person acting or feeling upset, then you can take the next step—identifying the characteristic way that an individual responds when difficulties arise. Sometimes exploring things in this order makes it easier for people to communicate freely about the things that they feel or the ways that they respond when difficulties arise (because *everyone* has bad days and gets upset). In my opinion, it is not critical to clearly distinguish between what people think or feel and the ways that they may visibly act when they become emotional. Nor is it important to encourage people to use certain words when they are speaking about themselves, their thoughts, or their actions. However, it is important to pay very special attention to the ways people act when they become upset. If you want to be in a position to help, you often need to be able to *see* these actions taking place in order to know when your help is needed.

It is usually true that people (particularly those who are likely to ask for help) have a characteristic way of acting when difficult life situations occur. In fact, difficult situations can bring out the very best and the very worst in all of us. Objective Three outlines the four general ways that a person can respond when the going gets tough (i.e., escape/avoid, withdraw/freeze, get emotional, or problem solve). This objective is intended to help dissect the characteristic way that an individual responds so that you can get in the best position to help. It may help if you dissect your own characteristic response before attempting to assist someone else with the process, although it is not really that difficult. The point is to identify as many markers as possible between the very first emotional signal and the most troublesome behavior that either has or could occur. Another name for this characteristic way of acting when the going gets difficult is an *emotional or behavioral sequence* (see Figure 1).

It is usually easy for most people to identify their first emotional signal of upset. People almost always pick out some physical feeling or sensation that they notice, such as breathing more quickly, twirling their hair, getting tense in the stomach or neck, becoming tearful, quivering, or blushing. I knew one man who reported that his first sign of upset was when he began to rub his tongue back and forth across the inside of his upper front teeth. Although simply asking a question (e.g., "What is your first sign of feeling upset?") is great for people who can communicate

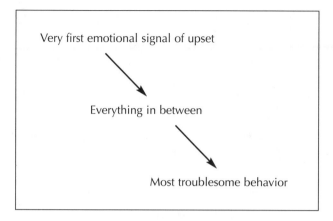

Figure 1. A characteristic sequence of responding to difficulties.

clearly, it may be more difficult for you to identify signs of upset for people who can't—their signs are often internal and you can't count on individuals without speech to have any existing vocabulary to help themselves or you identify the signs. Nevertheless, if you listen closely with all of your senses, you can usually identify these signals quite clearly for most individuals. Facial discoloration, rapid breathing, pacing, and particular sounds may be readily apparent to many potential helpers. Yet, although such signs may be useful to helpers, they may serve no signaling function whatsoever to the individual who is having difficulty. Sometimes when this problem is apparent, photographs can be useful to depict feelings or sensations that individuals may experience. For example, individuals who have a difficult time with identifying or labeling their feelings may be taught to point to pictures that depict certain feelings. Byron's story, later in this objective, illustrates this strategy well.

It is important to watch for the very first signal of upset very closely because many times people in need of help miss it, too (e.g., in the same way they might miss recognizing the situation or event that produced it). In fact, because they may not have been paying attention to such small signs, they may not notice that they are feeling anything at all until well into an emotional sequence. Sometimes the sequence appears to start with a thought. This can really make creating a list of signals tricky because thoughts can't be observed, but include them in the sequence anyway. After some simple analysis, you may be able to identify a half dozen or so different pieces of the characteristic emotional and behavioral sequence that occurs when difficulties arise. The real objective is to identify as many different pieces of the sequence as possible. The more you have, the more likely you may be able to help.

Identify Desired Actions

The third key part of a personal intervention plan is identifying desired actions or ways that are likely to be more effective in reducing the difficulties that an individual may be having. This section of the plan represents the better ways, desired actions, needed substitutes, or replacements for the characteristic ways that the person has used in the past. If possible, it should include actions that you have noticed an individual take at times in the past when the difficult situations did not produce any upsets. The key question here is something like, "What do you need to do instead when you notice that a difficult situation has arisen or that one of your signs of impending upset is present?" In many ways, this set of replacement actions is the personal intervention plan. This is what a person plans to do in the future when he or she notices that a situation has gotten difficult. This is what you will ask others to encourage you to do when they are helping you and, hopefully, what you will eventually be able to do on a more regular basis for yourself.

Sometimes, identification of desired actions is pretty easy. Certain individuals will be able to help identify some of the things that they may be doing already, such as taking deep breaths, counting to 10, maintaining silence, temporarily excusing themselves from a tough situation, thinking distracting thoughts, and perhaps most important, talking to themselves in a way that helps them stay calm and potentially solve the problem. Of course, individuals may do many other things in an attempt to handle their difficult situations. You can learn about them by asking and observing.

A few tips may help guide the development of this part of the plan. First, as with all of helping, the development of the plan should be as participatory as possible. Recognizing situations or events that produce difficulty, identifying existing emotional or behavioral sequences, and identifying different ways to reduce the difficulties should all involve interaction between yourself and the person you wish to help. This is not intended to be a directive process, unless the person you are helping has explicitly invited you to direct them. You are an idea generator, a resource, a teacher, a coach, a person who helps make the relationships between events and their consequences clearer, a participant in a mutually reinforcing exchange that (above all else) needs to be maintained. Second, as much as possible, all language or symbols that are used in the plan should be relevant to the person who is receiving the help. Remember that you are assisting in the development of that person's plan, not yours. Third, plans can change. They are not intended to be developed and then left alone. New situations, signs, and actions can be added at any time. Fourth, the plan probably ought to be reflected by some permanent product. Writing out or drawing the plan can be useful to the person in need of help as a tool for when life gets difficult, and it is also useful to the helper who may need to provide specific support or advice at particular times. When the desired actions specified on the plan become more automatic or when difficulties have been reduced, the permanent product may just serve as a reminder of a great relationship between the individuals who were involved in its creation.

Identify the Help That Is Needed

This is the last key part of the plan: identifying the help that is needed in order to use the plan effectively to manage the difficulties that arise. This section tends to vary more between individuals than the other parts of the plan because each individual has learned to be responsive to different types of help. What will it take for an individual to be able to act differently in the future, to use the new actions that have been identified, and to get the support he or she needs from others when a situation gets really difficult and when perhaps there is some danger on the horizon? This part of the plan includes *who* is going to help and *how* they are expected to help.

Hopefully, everyone has at least one person to include in the plan. This can be any person whom the individual has identified as someone to interact with when the individual is having difficulty acting for him- or herself. Ideally, the person would be someone who is often physically present and has a mutually reinforcing relationship with the individual, or someone who can watch for the difficult situations or emotional signals that the individual has identified in other parts of the plan. This person offers another set of eyes.

The helper is primarily there to encourage the individual to use the actions that he or she has identified in the previous section of the plan. This is where you can see two major differences between helping within a personal intervention structure and other ways of attempting to treat people. Because the replacement behaviors or actions are *desired* steps that the individual has identified, the helper's role becomes one of encouraging, prompting, reminding, and (most important) reinforcing the use of those actions, rather than solely discouraging ones that are not preferred.

Second, rather than being reactive just when the most difficult behaviors arise, a primary intention of personal intervention plans is to be *proactive* by encouraging intervention as early in the emotional or behavioral sequence as possible. This is why you should look so hard for the first signs in the sequence. Encouraging early intervention at the first sign of difficulty is important because it is more difficult to help an individual learn new behaviors when he or she is in the midst of intense emotional arousal that may affect his or her ability to think well and utilize support from others. In general, people are much more prepared to learn and solve problems when they are most calm. You need to be ready as early in the sequence as necessary to encourage use of the effective alternatives. "Striking when the iron is hot" is not consistent with a personal intervention approach.

Figure 2 provides a very simple outline of how a personal intervention plan can look. (A personal intervention plan can take many different forms, not just written.) As you can see, it is not really intended to be a complex or lengthy document, although some individuals may prefer to construct it that way. On the contrary, if it is relatively simple, it may be clearer, more applicable, and more useful during difficult life situations.

I learned many of these things about personal intervention from a young man named Byron. Byron was a big, strong, young man who lived in a very restricted living situation mostly for people who were diagnosed with developmental disabilities who could become very aggressive. He was typically silent around others even when he appeared to be doing well. If he became upset, however, it seemed that he very rapidly got to the point of seriously damaging the residence or other people in it. At the time we met, he was about to be transferred to a correctional facility—a move that would have resulted in an even greater loss of independence in his life.

Contrary to what I had been told to expect, I found it relatively easy to establish a mutually reinforcing relationship with Byron. I did this by interacting with him in a scheduled way for brief periods of time every day I worked. I would also make a point to interact more informally every time I would pass him or see him in the distance. I did my best to have our interactions stand out for Byron in a positive, upbeat way so that he might perceive them as being noticeably different from those he seemed to be having with so many others. I tried to look calm and collected even though I was often very apprehensive and on

**A Simple Personal
Intervention Plan for** _____

This plan is intended to assist you (and those who may help you) to learn more about yourself and get better at managing your emotions and behavior when difficult situations arise. Consider it a representation of ways you have acted in the past and a new start on ways you wish to act in your future.

1a. I am likely to have a bad day when...
     (List at least three situations that may precede a bad day.)

1b. I am likely to get upset when...
     *(List at least five events that produce
     emotional or behavioral upsets for you.)*

2.   When I get emotionally upset, I notice a sequence that starts
     with _____ and may end with _____ .
     *(Make a list from the very first sign
     to other things that do or could occur.)*

3.   When I notice that a difficult situation is
     coming or when I begin to get emotionally
     upset, I will have the most success when I...
     (List the steps you need to take.)

4.   Other people can help me at these times by...
     *(Identify who you need to help
     and list what you need them to do.)*

Figure 2.   A sample outline for a personal intervention plan.

guard during our first interactions. When we could, we would have our scheduled meetings in a separate place away from his living situation. This opportunity seemed to be pretty special to Byron. I asked him over and over about things I knew he liked and showed him some of my personal things, such as pictures that I had around my office. To the extent possible, we would meet regardless of how he had been behaving that day. Given the positive nature of our interactions, Byron never resisted meeting or interacting with me. For a while, I did my best not to bring up any problem or situation that he might perceive as difficult.

At the point that I was comfortable that Byron valued our interaction and would seek it out, I slowly began to have him teach me some of what he knew about himself. For example, I started to ask him how he was doing that day or if he was having any problems. I tried to learn about what he felt like if he was (what I referred to as) sad or bored. I finally asked him about his anger and his attacks on the people he lived with. Overall, I gradually exposed Byron to increasingly difficult topics and tasks so that I would not tip the balance and jeopardize the relationship we had developed.

The most important thing I learned was that Byron seemed to know very little about himself. He had no words or expressions for most of the things he felt. He appeared to have a full range of emotions, but he had no way of relating these emotions to any of the things that happened around him or to him. He had no way understand the connection between these emotions and the things he did or might do. He had no way of identifying these emotions to others who might be in a position to help him. Because of these problems, I concluded that he was not yet in a position to be helped and others were not yet in a position to help him. He had very few mutually reinforcing exchanges where he lived. He did not resist help, he just had so little experience with it. I needed to maintain our interactions so that I could assume more of a teaching role.

It appeared that Byron needed to learn to interpret what he was feeling so that he could communicate more effectively and so that others could get in a better position to help him when he was having a difficult time. In an attempt to address this problem, I started by taking pictures of Byron making all sorts of faces: smiling faces, blank faces, frowning faces. Byron really liked having his picture taken and then looking at the photos. In order to maintain a balance between our history of positive interactions and my increased expectations, we eventually agreed to put words next to his pictures. These were simple words like "happy," "okay," "sad," "angry," and "mad." Because he still had trouble at times matching these words to the different pictures, we worked on just three pictures and the new words that we decided went with them. I also put colored backgrounds on the pictures and words, so that maybe if he didn't recognize the word or the face, he would recognize the color as a signal. Eventually we clarified Byron's feelings as happy, okay, and mad with the corresponding pictures of himself looking these ways and the colors green, yellow, and red in each of the respective backgrounds. I viewed this as a very important accomplishment for Byron, and we had a great time putting everything we had learned about his emotions on one narrow strip of paper with plastic over it that he could carry in his new wallet. We got to the point that I could meet him, ask how he was doing, and he would show me on his picture board, which he seemed very proud of. I was sure that he liked the board so much because it reminded him of some of the mutually reinforcing interactions we had experienced.

During this learning time, many people began to notice a change in Byron. He was already behaving less aggressively and seemed to be less threatening for others to be around. But it wasn't enough. He could communicate with others using his pictures, but it really didn't help Byron or others know what to do when he reported that he felt a particular way.

In order to encourage particular interactions when he reported his feelings, Byron and I continued our learning process about personal intervention. This time, we added another picture for each feeling that represented what we agreed we would do together if he reported feeling one way or the other. Next to "Smiling-Happy-Green" was a photo of several potential helpers clapping, smiling, and patting Byron on the back. Next to "Blank-Okay-Yellow," we put a picture of Byron sitting in his room. For "Frowning-Mad-Red," we created a picture of helpers standing with Byron holding the belt and cuff restraints that he was so familiar with. In the past, these devices had been used *after* he had become aggressive, usually for several hours or even days at a time. Using them was not really what anyone preferred, but unfortunately it did represent Byron's experience and the remarkable danger he could present when he became aggressive. Part of the plan was to eliminate the need for such interventions in Byron's future.

As we continued learning, we practiced each one of these outcomes after I would encourage Byron to point to one or the other of the signs. I continued to try to make practicing fun and to have him participate as much as possible in the process, right down to helping me put the restraints on him when he pointed to "Frowning-Mad-Red." If Byron got to this point in the past, it was a sure sign that he would become aggressive in a danger-ous way within a very short time. To get him to participate in taking the measures that appeared necessary to help him control himself was particularly unusual and encouraging because Byron was often the most dangerous when these devices were being applied. Although he would strongly resist others' attempts to physically control him, perhaps he might become a participant in controlling himself, a major objective of per-sonal intervention.

After we had fun practicing over and over, it was time for other potential helpers to participate in assisting Byron to man-age his emotions and behavior more autonomously and effec-tively. To this end, others were asked to check with Byron each hour, using his signal board, as he went through his day to see how he was doing. I also informed them that Byron now expected them to help him take the actions that were identified for each emotion on the board (e.g., clap, smile, and pat him on the back; encourage him to sit in his room; prepare to help him apply restraints). If he reported "Blank-Okay-Yellow" or "Frowning-Mad-Red," Byron had learned that he was to take the actions on the board until he could again report that he was "Smiling-Happy-Green." This was part of the plan to encourage his early intervention, before he might become dangerous. Although other potential helpers were occasionally hesitant to use the approach that Byron had helped create and used it inconsistently, Byron enjoyed the longest period with no aggression in his life, and plans to transfer him to a correctional facility were dropped.

This is a good example of how to use the personal intervention way of thinking, organizing, and planning because it demonstrates several other underlying points. First, it is not necessary for a person to be identified as functioning at a particular level in order to use this type of strategy. A plan can probably be adapted for virtually any individual's situation. Second, it is not critical that every part of the plan be developed to the same degree of complexity. In Byron's situation, we never did really focus on when he was likely to have a bad day or the specific events that were likely to make him upset. These things were diverse and highly variable, and it is unlikely that he would have been able to learn how to identify and communicate them effectively. Third, a plan is expected to be flexible and dynamic. Byron's plan changed as needed to accommodate new issues that arose. Finally, although a plan is likely to develop out of a single mutually reinforcing relationship, in most circumstances it will need to be shared with other potential helpers in order to be useful. In many situations in which I have been involved, the plan has been used as a vital and very public part of the treatment, habilitation, or rehabilitation plan that was used by a whole team of potential helpers. In fact, in a situation such as Byron's, it can be useful to create opportunities for the person to instruct others about his or her plan rather than having a helper do this. Having the person instruct others seems to instill an increased sense of personal ownership in the plan and, of course, provides more opportunities for practice.

☐ ☐ ☐ ☐ ☐ ☐

Another amazing thing happened. I attended our regional Special Olympics because an agency for which I worked was a sponsor of the event. As I was walking through the crowd trying to find a seat, I heard someone call my name from many rows up in the stands. To my surprise and delight, it was Byron. I hustled up the steps and greeted him with a huge hug, although I'm not sure we had ever hugged before. He remembered me! He knew my name! He was thrilled to see me even though it had been 9 years since we had seen each other. I have little doubt that this memory will stay with me for a long time.

SUMMARY

The overall purpose of your help is to better prepare an individual for the difficult situations that he or she may face in life. One general manner of providing help that embodies this purpose within a problem-solving, self-control, or functional communication approach is called *personal intervention.* In the simplest terms, personal intervention is an individualized strategy for living when difficulties arise. It consists of four primary parts including 1) recognizing when an individual is likely to experience difficulty, 2) identifying the characteristic sequence of emotional and behavioral responding when difficulties arise, 3) identifying desired actions that are likely to reduce the difficulties, and 4) identifying the help that is needed when an individual can't or doesn't act effectively on his or her own. To some extent, personal intervention is what we all do when we experience difficulties and we could probably all get better at it.

Recognizing that the purpose of your help is to promote individuals' independence and that the personal intervention structure may be a useful manner of organizing your help is part of what can be referred to as *proactive treatment.* Proactive treatment refers to all of the things you may do in order to assist an individual to be ready for the difficult situations that may arise in his or her life. It makes sense to approach helping in a proactive way for many reasons. First, it allows for greater participation from the person in need of help. Second, it puts potential helpers in the role of strengthening desired personal intervention skills, rather than simply discouraging certain ways of acting when difficulties arise. Third, it may allow for earlier intervention in situations that could turn ugly or even dangerous and thus ultimately reduce risks. Fourth, it is intended to take advantage of a greater likelihood for individual learning by introducing help at lower levels of emotional arousal. People don't generally learn or solve problems very well when they are in the midst of intense emotions. And finally, it puts the potential helper in a coaching role (to use effective action) rather than an adversarial one. This last reason may help you be able to maintain a mutually reinforcing exchange even during very troubling situations.

Bounce Off the Upsets

A helper usually notices that a potential helping situation exists when someone he or she is in contact with experiences difficulty and then behaves in a way that is not considered to be acceptable or preferred. It would be great if you didn't have to wait for the emotional and behavioral signs of upset to occur before providing help (e.g., imagine a school curriculum for children that focused on teaching personal intervention skills), but for whatever reason, the world doesn't work that way very often.

Because upsets (i.e., behaviors described as unwanted, problematic, or challenging) signal the presence of a difficult life situation, it is not particularly surprising that *reducing* these behaviors has frequently become the focus of helping efforts. It seems to be easier to see what is wrong, what needs to be corrected, or what needs to be stopped than it is to see what is going well, what can be strengthened, or what skill needs to be enhanced to make life go a little more smoothly. It is particularly difficult to see what is going well when an individual becomes upset over and over again during a short period of time. In my opinion, however, being able to recognize the difference between reducing unwanted behaviors and strengthening desired skills as ways of approaching the helping situation is absolutely critical;

your understanding of this difference is likely to affect the ways that you attempt to help.

When you approach a helping situation from a perspective of just stopping an upset, you can be unexpectedly drawn or even naturally inclined to particular ways of providing help. From a behavioral perspective, many people seem to focus on two primary approaches when they try to get something to stop. First, you can take an action following the particular behavior that is intended to reduce its chance of happening again in the future. This is often what is intended when people correct, say "stop that," reprimand, give a discouraging look, spank, take away privileges, or throw a person in jail following the display of some troubling behavior. The belief is that by doing one or more of these things, the chance of that behavior happening again will be reduced. And, of course, sometimes it is.

The second way people attempt to stop an upset is by trying to not pay any attention to it. The belief here is that by not following the behavior with attention or a potential desired inter-action of some kind, it is less likely to occur again. A helper may believe that this is *why* the upset is occurring in the first place (e.g., to get someone's much desired attention). Sometimes, a behavior can represent a request for attention, and not paying attention will reduce the likelihood of it being repeated in the future. In these situations, a person might conclude that the attention-seeking behavior stops because it no longer pays off.

Introducing some presumed unwanted consequence follow-ing an upset may reduce its chance of happening again, but sometimes this doesn't work. Similarly, a helper may believe that taking away his or her valuable attention following the behavior will reduce its chance of happening again, but some-times this also doesn't work. As discussed in Objective One, doing either of these things very often makes matters much worse. Misuse of these common ways of interacting probably accounts for many of the most serious problems that occur in this world due to the attack–attack reciprocity phenomenon.

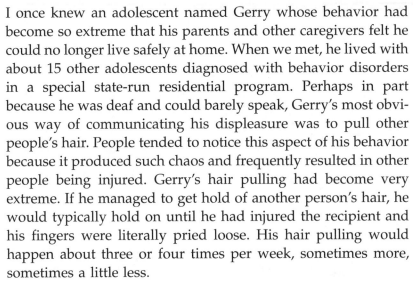

I once knew an adolescent named Gerry whose behavior had become so extreme that his parents and other caregivers felt he could no longer live safely at home. When we met, he lived with about 15 other adolescents diagnosed with behavior disorders in a special state-run residential program. Perhaps in part because he was deaf and could barely speak, Gerry's most obvious way of communicating his displeasure was to pull other people's hair. People tended to notice this aspect of his behavior because it produced such chaos and frequently resulted in other people being injured. Gerry's hair pulling had become very extreme. If he managed to get hold of another person's hair, he would typically hold on until he had injured the recipient and his fingers were literally pried loose. His hair pulling would happen about three or four times per week, sometimes more, sometimes a little less.

At the time, people who might have helped, including me, thought that we had tried everything to get Gerry to stop pulling hair. We had corrected him, we had given him special things for not pulling hair, we had taught him how to request to be excused from difficult tasks, and we had put him in seclusion following his attacks. We had put him in restraints and mittens as consequences and later just as a way to try to keep everyone safe. Nothing really worked to reduce Gerry's hair pulling, and all of the potential helpers were at their wit's end.

Following the belief that we could find some consequence that would reduce the future probability of these behaviors, we received various levels of permission to take some really extraordinary steps. We received permission to pop ammonia capsules under Gerry's nose if he had someone by the hair. We received permission to spray him in the face with water mist. We received permission to deliver electric shock from either remote-controlled or hand-held shocking devices that were more typically used for animals. All of these consequences were intended to get Gerry to stop pulling other people's hair.

To summarize what occurred, these measures produced a drastic, expected, and immediate *increase* in Gerry's aggressiveness and hair pulling. For nearly a week, he was attacking on a regular basis, and on some days, he would receive hundreds of electric shocks, occasionally while being physically held and simultaneously receiving ammonia pops and water mist. There was no question that during this period, Gerry became more aggressive than he had ever been. He fought back in ways no one had ever seen him do: spitting, kicking, biting, yelling, and crying. I had never broken a horse, but it seemed like this is what we were attempting to do. We carried on and on.

Then, it happened. After about 2 weeks of this very intensive, all-day training that involved several full-time helpers to conduct, there was calm. Gerry stopped fighting back. He began to follow most of the instructions that were given to him. He got to go to McDonald's. He got to go home on Thanksgiving. He went to work almost every day at a local workshop for people with special needs. The news seemed good as long as the main signal, the shock device, was present. There was a great sense that we had helped this young man have a much fuller life. There was also a strange sense of impending doom that is still very difficult to describe. It was as if most of us knew that it wouldn't actually last. Gerry would probably start getting upset and pulling hair again. Of course he would. We would be back in the ring again. It was just a matter of time.

In spite of several very creative attempts to maintain the improvements, over the course of the next 2 years, Gerry's hair pulling slowly and steadily increased to about the frequency and intensity that it had been prior to the introduction of the special procedures: a few times per week, sometimes more, sometimes less. Gradually, the potential helpers faded away. Gradually, all of the procedures were dropped (because they didn't work well at that point anyway and no one was willing to advocate for reintroduction of the intensive training). Gradually, Gerry's life began to look very much like it had prior to the whole experience. He lost his opportunity to participate at the local workshop, he didn't go to McDonald's, and he didn't visit his family any more often than he ever had.

People can and do learn as a result of consequences that are delivered after they have become upset. However, it is reasonable to wonder what it is that they may be learning. Sometimes treating people in this reactive way reduces troubling behaviors as planned, but many times it won't. When it doesn't, it may inadvertently make matters much worse. Sometimes treating people in this way can lead to more frequent, intense, or durable displays of emotional behavior and *less* likelihood that others will ever get themselves in a position to help in some other, less dramatic way.

Many people I know who have grown up in an ongoing exchange of attack–attack interactions are, as a result, very difficult to help. I don't believe that they see that anyone intends to provide any help. The same is often true when a helper attempts to withhold his or her attention when people display problem behaviors. Let's say that George decides that he is going to ignore Sharon, who lives in her own apartment in the community, when she displays her typical signs of becoming upset. He knows in advance that, if he does this, several negative things may happen. First, she may begin to do whatever she is doing more often. Second, she may do whatever it is more intensely. Third, she may behave in new ways that are even more troubling. Finally, she may discover ways to get what she wants (as if that was a bad thing) somewhere or from someone else.

Situations could arise from withholding attention that may lead the helper into more trouble. There may be situations where you simply cannot withhold your attention. For example, suppose that Sharon usually lets George know that she is in a difficult life situation by calling him at work for a little advice or encouragement. George wants her to stop doing this, so he decides not to take calls from her while he is at work. Then one day, he finds himself on the phone with Sharon's neighbor who is sitting with Sharon trying to console her. Sharon has now developed a new behavior in order to maintain what had been a reinforcing interaction for her prior to George's change of heart. George senses that if he takes the call, he may now be encouraging Sharon's new way of getting what she desires: his attention. George may be getting upset. George is in a dilemma.

George decides to hold out. Nothing has changed for Sharon. She still has difficulties and she still looks to George for help, except now he is beginning to expect more action from her before he permits her to have what she desires. The next time Sharon experiences difficulties, George refuses her call and her neighbor's call. He still thinks that withholding his attention will ultimately reduce this annoying request for his help. Shortly thereafter, he gets a call from his 10-year-old daughter, Lucy, who says that Sharon is at their house. Although Lucy is trying to calm Sharon down, Lucy wants his help in the matter. George holds out again because he doesn't want to teach Sharon to go to his daughter or his house to get help.

George tells his daughter to let Sharon know that he is going to call the police if Sharon doesn't leave the house. She leaves, but her sequence of emotional and behavioral responses does not stop. Thirty minutes later, George gets a call from the local police informing him that his help is needed to talk Sharon down from the roof of the building where he works. Considering the magnitude of the risk at this point, George finally agrees to interact with Sharon.

Although this example may seem absurd, there is a very recognizable element of truth in it. Many helpers have tried this strategy and have found themselves in situations that escalate like this. Of course, sometimes withholding attention works. But sometimes the problems continue, intensify, and endure through well-intentioned efforts to reduce them by withholding attention. It is important to understand that there is a very good reason for this result. In Sharon's attention-seeking situation, for example, it appears that George was gradually and inadvertently teaching her to respond differently in order to get his attention. She was just doing the best she could (considering her existing skills) to maintain what she may have desired. In fact, George was accidentally using one of the most powerful teaching procedures known: positive reinforcement.

Positive reinforcement is an event that follows a particular behavior and increases the chances that the behavior will occur again. Although George didn't plan for it to happen that way, Sharon continued to be positively reinforced for behaving in different ways in order to secure what she needed. His own beliefs about the way things are supposed to work got in the way. If a helper doesn't provide attention after a problem behavior, shouldn't it go away? The answer is almost always maybe. Maybe ignoring the behavior will make it worse. Many terrible accidents have occurred as a result of beliefs about how things are supposed to work. The truth is that people really don't know how strategies will work until they put the strategies to the test. This is another hallmark of science.

One of helping's main objectives is to do no harm, yet helpers can very possibly make difficult situations worse when they use consequences or withholding attention in an attempt to reduce behaviors associated with upsets. So, what should you do instead? The answer is probably one of the most important messages of this book: You should *attempt to strengthen desired behaviors using positive reinforcement.* In Sharon's situation, this may mean sitting down with her, ensuring the presence of a mutually reinforcing pattern of interactions, developing a personal intervention plan that includes actions that Sharon may take short of calling you on the phone at work, and then identifying how you can help Sharon use these replacement behaviors more effectively in her future. It is very likely that adopting this strategy will involve the introduction of events intended to increase and encourage the use of these desired behaviors (i.e., positive reinforcers).

Causing harm is much more difficult using positive reinforcers to increase desired behavior than it is when you use consequences or withholding attention to reduce unwanted

behavior. If you miss an opportunity to provide a positive reinforcer, you are probably as likely to produce an increase in the
desired actions as you are to encourage reemergence of the
behavior you want to reduce. You will be less likely to do harm
using this strategy. Think about it. If you are receiving regular
acknowledgement from your supervisor for doing your work
and then he or she misses one or two opportunities to acknowledge you, you are not very likely to stop doing the things that
get acknowledged. You may even do a little more of the work
just to make sure he or she is paying attention. Reinforcers,
however, should be put to the test as well. A helper can't assume
that some particular event will act to increase an action without
testing it first.

Jermaine is a young man diagnosed with autism who has limited
communication skills and may become upset when abrupt
changes are made in his environment. His helper, Gloria, would
like to select good reinforcers to use in a personal intervention
plan that is intended to increase his skill of looking away or
covering his eyes (which he has done on his own several times
in the past), rather than running off or injuring himself when
difficulties arise. She has heard how much Jermaine likes to
go out to restaurants for hamburgers, and she assumes that
providing an opportunity to go to McDonald's could increase
Jermaine's personal intervention skills. She devises a program
in which Jermaine is to receive one fourth of a picture of a
McDonald's restaurant each time he displays the desired behavior in a situation in which upset might have occurred. A full
picture of McDonald's equals a trip to the restaurant the following day.

   Although Gloria has used some good skills in her program
design, she is very surprised when the plan has no impact on
the frequency of Jermaine's desired behavior or upsets. As a

result, she modifies the photo pieces of McDonald's several times, repeatedly practices the desired responses with Jermaine, and even gives him one piece of the photo to begin with, just to see if she can get the program started. It is at this point that *Gloria* learns something very important. Jermaine takes the piece and deposits it in the garbage can. When Gloria sees this, she immediately gets out some magazines, cuts out pictures of different restaurants, and encourages Jermaine to point to one that he prefers. The program goes quite well after that interaction. The moral of the story is that although Jermaine likes going to restaurants for hamburgers, McDonald's hamburgers are unlikely to serve as a reinforcer for any of his behaviors.

There are lots of other things that some people may like or desire that will not always function as reinforcers to increase any of their behaviors. Food is a good reinforcer for many, but it loses its effectiveness at times when a person has already had enough. A pat on the back is a great idea for a lot of people, but I know others who will do all sorts of unusual things to avoid having one at certain times. Money is a good reinforcer because it can be exchanged for so many other desired things. However, I know many people who would be more likely to throw it away than they would be to spend it on things they might desire. Some of these individuals have not learned the relationship between money and what they may desire.

In order to understand the effect of a particular event on another person's behavior (i.e., whether it will increase or decrease a behavior), you cannot just follow your hunches, assumptions, or beliefs about the way it *should* be or even about the way it is for most people. A helper has to act a bit more like a scientist and put these relationships to the test. This means observing what happens to the frequency, intensity, or length of time that a behavior occurs when it is followed by a particular event. You already know that people have all sorts of reasons or causes for behaving like they do, and it is within your helping role to learn more about them. It is pretty difficult to consistently count on anything. This is another reason why acting in ways that are likely to keep interaction going is a really good guideline for helping. People change, and as a helper, you need to change with them if you expect to remain in a position to help.

The phrase "bounce off the upsets" is intended to encourage you to refrain from devoting too much of your attention to what happens when people become very upset and instead to focus on the situations or events that produce these actions. In some ways, it may be useful to consider that the emotions or behaviors an individual may display during an intense upset are not really the problems at all. The problem is that the individual may not have a more effective way to respond to the difficulty that has arisen for him or her at the time. Your task, as a helper, is to do your best to manage the risks that intense upsets may involve, restore calm, and get back to interacting in a way that is likely to encourage effective alternatives as rapidly as possible, using positive reinforcers.

Learning how to assist someone during an upset, particularly when it becomes very intense or potentially dangerous, is largely about acting in ways that are intended to keep the person's excitement level as low as possible. The less excited someone is, the more likely the person is able to use his or her personal intervention skills and your assistance. The less excited someone is, the more likely he or she is to be able to think and problem solve more effectively. Most people understand that they don't think as clearly or act as sensibly when they are very upset. Remember that your primary objectives are to keep people as safe as possible, to reduce the excitement level, and to encourage other ways to address whatever is causing the problem. To do this, you must have a great deal of tolerance, which comes with realistic preparation for helping and trusting that people are doing the best they can even when it may not appear that way. To do this, you must also intervene as early in the sequence of emotional and behavioral upsets as possible in order to encourage use of more effective personal intervention strategies with positive reinforcers.

DE-ESCALATION APPROACHES

If you find yourself in a situation in which the person you are attempting to assist is either very likely to become seriously upset or if he or she is already very upset, consider the following six de-escalation approaches. Sometimes these approaches can be used separately, but learning to use them well often involves using parts of several of these approaches within the same episode, almost at the same time.

Priming

Many individuals are likely to become upset when they are instructed, asked, or commanded to do something, particularly something that is hard for them to do. When you are preparing to interact with a person who is likely to have big problems when you make a particular request, it is usually not a very good idea to start by making the request. Similarly, telling a person who is already upset to just stop acting like that can very often makes the situation worse. These situations can place your history of mutually reinforcing interactions with the individual at risk. The key here is to establish interaction that is not focused directly on the difficult request. In fact, try to resist the inclination or temptation to be drawn into an interaction that focuses on it. *Priming* is an approach in which you attempt to have two or three neutral, unrelated, or positive interactions with an individual before you make any requests that may be difficult for them.

Jason almost always gets upset when he is asked to put his dishes away after dinner. Before making that request, Ann has a casual conversation with Jason by talking about the weather, where she went over the weekend, and so forth. After she can predict that she has established a neutral or positive interaction with Jason, she makes the difficult request and offers to help in any way that she can. If Jason doesn't respond favorably, Ann doesn't get excited; she just repeats the approach.

Topic Dispersal

In the midst of very intense emotional upset, sometimes people seem to get stuck or perseverate on whatever it is that is making them upset. Of course, this just serves to keep the emotions rolling, almost like fuel on a fire. In your efforts to help, you can sometimes mistakenly encourage this by interacting about the event while the person is in the throes of his or her difficulties. Instead, distract the focus from this event to produce some calm. *Topic dispersal* is an approach in which you introduce several different topics in rapid succession to encourage the person to pause and break up or disperse the pattern of thought.

When Ginny gets really emotional, she locks in on a particular phrase about her mother that she repeats over and over. Because this usually precedes a very intense crying bout that can last for hours, when Juan hears this, he starts making comments about her favorite TV shows, birds, what's for dinner, and last Christmas, almost all at the same time. These are all topics that might catch Ginny's attention because she has talked about them before, and Juan knows from experience he can help Ginny restore calm by doing this. He wouldn't do it, of course, if he knew it would make Ginny more confused.

Focused Redirection

Some people tend to shift from topic to topic when they become emotional, almost as if they have temporarily lost their ability to focus on the difficulty they are experiencing at the time. *Focused redirection* is an approach in which the helper attempts to pick out a relevant segment of a very confusing verbalization and focus the interaction on that piece of the communication.

John becomes very urgent during an upset, and his words ramble from thought to thought to thought in a repetitious and almost frantic way. Shondra has a pretty characteristic way of interacting with John at these times. She picks out a particular piece of his verbal content and directs questions to that part until he begins to focus more clearly. Later, she helps him with whatever situation made him upset in the first place.

Reinforcer Recall

When experiencing very intense emotions, people sometimes seem to forget their mutually reinforcing history of interactions with a person who may be attempting to assist them. *Reinforcer recall* is an approach in which the helper uses a very high rate of positive interaction during times of calm and then reminds the person in need of assistance about one or more of these interactions when they become upset.

Marcus always interacts positively with Jordan, collecting what some would call *interactional money in the bank* with Jordan because of this. Whenever Jordan has difficulty managing his emotions, Marcus can usually just remind him of something great they have done together and then help him with difficult situations very quickly. Marcus has noticed that people who have not had a history of positive interactions with Jordan don't have anything to "cash in" when he is upset.

Personal Intervention, Functional Replacement, and Behavioral Momentum

When people become upset, they often need to be encouraged to use some other set of skills to handle their emotions, solve their problem, or both. As mentioned in Objective Five, helping people learn useful personal intervention skills can be an effective strategy. *Personal intervention* is a label for a set of approaches to plan out these actions in advance so that, when difficulty arises, two or more people can work together to use the actions they have identified. *Functional replacement* is a very similar strategy wherein a helper encourages desired actions that are equally effective for the individual to solve his or her dilemma. *Behavioral momentum* is an approach in which a helper simplifies his or her requests to the point that the person in trouble can and will respond favorably and then provides encouragement for doing so.

Margie has been in a helping role with Chris for a long time. They have talked about a lot about events including the difficulties that produce upset for Chris, what it is like (from start to finish) when he becomes upset, what Chris would really like to be able to do instead when he becomes upset, and the ways he has identified in which Margie can help him when tough situations arise. The two have agreed that one of the most important things that Margie can do when Chris is really upset is to ask him to make eye contact with her first. After he makes eye contact, she acknowledges this *desired* response (e.g., "Thanks for looking at me, Chris") and then proceeds through helping steps that include coaching him to briefly step away from what made him upset, engage in some distracting activity, and then problem solve other ways to confront the situation if it ever arises again. Because Margie usually helps Chris early in his sequence of reactions and before things escalate, it is clear that a very effective helping and learning relationship has been established.

I used a combination of these procedures with the young woman whom I met at the rehabilitation hospital (see Objective Three). Recall that this woman began screaming, shouting profanities, and throwing things at the beginning of our very first interaction together. She had good reasons to act like that, considering her history, and I guessed that her intention or purpose with these behaviors was to get me to leave the room. Acting on this simple analysis, I began to repeat the phrase, "If you want me to leave, just ask me to leave," as she continued to shout at me. Finally, after I had calmly repeated this request about six or so times, she screamed, "Would you get the !*$? out of my room?" I figured that was good enough for her first try at a more suitable request, so I left.

That wasn't, however, the end of our interaction. In a minute or so, I tapped on the door and entered her room again. Just as before, she started screaming, questioning my heritage, and so on. I used the same request again, and she responded more quickly and quietly in her request for me to leave. I did. We went through this routine about five times before she gradually permitted me to stay in the room for longer periods before asking me to leave in a very reasonable manner. During the times I was in the room, I did my best to teach her my name, her name, where we were, and so on in a very repetitious way. I smiled a lot. By the end of our 3-hour visit, I had broken the hospital's record by being in her presence without being asked to leave or experiencing an aggressive response of any kind for more than 45 consecutive minutes. She even allowed me to assist her into a wheelchair and take her out of her room for the first time since she had been hospitalized. The development of a mutually reinforcing relationship was well underway as a result of understanding that there were good reasons for her behavior, not blaming her, listening to her closely, and bouncing off her upsets by using some fairly straightforward functional replacement approaches.

SUMMARY

Although I have often wished that it was not this way, usually helpers know that help is needed when they observe that someone else is upset. It is very important, however, to avoid the trap of simply trying to reduce or stop these upsets. This is because attempting to reduce emotional or behavioral problems by providing consequences or withholding attention may inadvertently result in greater problems, when the individual you are attempting to assist is not responsive to these approaches. Positive reinforcement of new ways to act in difficult situations is probably the clearest way to help, but remember that positive reinforcers are different for everybody. They must be put to the test to determine if they actually result in an increase in desired behaviors. Looking for these relationships can make helping very interesting. It may also make you more tolerant of the troubling behaviors that people may exhibit because you can recognize that they are really just doing the best they can with the skills that they have. If you can learn to approach upsets in this way, you can keep yourself in a position to help, even when very difficult situations arise, by using some simple de-escalation approaches.

Be Clear on the Purpose of Your Help

Over the years, various ways of helping have looked very different. For example, there is now a great deal of interest in the development and use of proactive treatment approaches. At the same time, there has been increased interest in providing the supports or accommodations that individuals may need in order to help them have success in the most independent living situations possible for them. The places where people have given and received help have changed as well. More and more individuals are receiving the help that they need in settings that are more integrated into their communities.

Even in light of these developments, differences continue to exist in how potential helpers view the ways and places that help is provided. Certainly, not all help is provided in a proactive way in a community-integrated setting. It may be important to briefly consider some of the history related to these issues so that you can be clearer about your own views regarding the purpose of your help. Doing so may help you better understand your role in a given situation and be better prepared to advocate for particular actions that may be useful for the individuals you are attempting to assist. Perhaps a quick look at human service history would help in making these sorts of decisions.

Helping usually has a cost, and funding agencies and other organizations (e.g., churches, parent and advocacy groups, foundations) have had to establish policies and practices regarding what types of help they are interested in supporting. In the early part of the 20th century, most people still believed that those who needed the most help should be cared for in a custodial way in special places called *institutions, schools, farms,* or *hospitals.* In fact, although hundreds of people may have lived together, some of these places were even called *homes.* In many ways, starting to call them *special* and *homes* may have confused things for a lot of people.

There is no question that the people who created these places and provided the help were usually caring individuals with good intentions. However, it started to become clear that the help that they provided often was not directed toward any particular outcome. It was not specifically intended to result in any desired change for the individual or to better prepare people for the difficult situations that might arise in their lives. It was often just intended to put a roof over people's heads, provide some nourishment, and give them a place to sleep. Perhaps this was exactly what some people needed.

In the past 30 years, there seems to have been a huge collective realization that this way of providing help for those who were in the most serious need was not really working. Suddenly, too many thousands of people were living in these situations. Many were communicating that it was not producing any desired change for them, and very few were becoming better equipped to handle troubling circumstances or to achieve greater independence in their lives. Incidences of abuse and neglect were seemingly endless (perhaps the result of ongoing attack–attack interactions), and caring for people in this way had become much too costly for the agencies and organizations to bear. These were all very good reasons for some things to change.

Looking very broadly at developments since the 1970s, you can see that at least four very important things changed that began to reflect a new attitude toward helping. First, community mental health legislation was passed that placed limits on who could be admitted and who could continue living in the existing places where public help was being provided. This change meant that many people who had been inappropriately placed were deinstitutionalized or moved to the community. Second, other legislation around issues of least restrictive treatment (people must be treated in the least restrictive place and manner possible) and active treatment (all help must be designed to enhance personal autonomy or independence), in addition to the Education for All Handicapped Children Act of 1975 (PL 94-142; public education shall be made available to everyone) and subsequent reauthorizations, further influenced where and even how help was to be provided. Third, remarkable energy and creativity was generated around the development of new ways to provide assistance to people, including the creation of a new technology currently called *behavior analysis,* important advancements in special education practices, the organization of new advocacy groups, volumes and volumes of new intervention literature, and so on. Finally, there appeared to be reasonable consensus that all of these things were making a very important and meaningful difference in the lives of individuals who were in need of help.

This short history lesson may be important because it accents the relative newness of more active ways of attempting to help people, provides perspective on some of the reasons why helping looks like it does at the start of the 21st century, and provides some markers that may influence the way that you actually help. It may seem as though the news is very good, and all helpers really need to do at this point is continue on the track they are on, keep doing the things that they currently know how to do, and enjoy the important progress that has been made in human services. Yet, as I hinted, it is still sometimes very difficult to tell if the glass of human service progress is half full or half empty. Although it is tempting to be moved by everything that has been accomplished, it is possible to be shaken at times by certain things that have not. In a general way, I think it may be important to consider some of these things as well.

"Budget Ax Falls on Disabled Students," a *Chicago Tribune* article, reported, "State health officials have begun shipping young, disabled students from the Illinois Center for Rehabilitation and Education to nursing homes as part of a plan to close the residential school and save $2.5 million in next year's budget" (2002, p. 1A). The story focused on a 21-year-old young man named Lorne, who would lose his access not only to educational opportunities that he had been receiving at the school but also to other mandated interventions that were intended to help him integrate into the community at some point in his future. According to the administrator of the nursing home where this young man was to be placed, Lorne would be "by far the youngest" and "highest cognitively functioning" of all of the residents at the home. The administrator also reported that the home was "full of older adults who have such severe mental impairments that they have been institutionalized all their lives." It was also reported, but not substantiated, that Lorne had been transported to the nursing home, which was 250 miles from his mother's home in Chicago, under the pretense that he could "check it out," but that after he got there, he was told he could not return to the center.

To me, this story and some of the language it contained seemed almost unimaginable in the year 2002. Although it may have been written in a way that was designed to produce a change in the situation for Lorne and his 50 classmates at the school, it described an incident that is not isolated or inconsistent with the experience of many families of people diagnosed with disabilities when they are attempting to find help. On any given day, many individuals continue to go without any help whatsoever, atrocities related to people who are in need of help continue to be reported and not reported, and many people find themselves in situations that are very unlikely to result in any sort of a positive outcome in their lives. This latter point is underscored by the fact that many existing institutional placements that had begun to focus on community integration have very recently been transformed or replaced with other institutional placements that do not have such expectations. These placements are often called *forensics, juvenile detention, corrections,* or *prisons*.

There is good news and bad news, depending on what you see and hear. Perhaps the most important thing to consider is what this information means. What should it mean for the well-intentioned individuals who may be in a position to help at the nursing home where Lorne may be placed? What should it mean for the individuals who wish to help in correctional settings or even in some community living situations where individuals in need of help may find themselves isolated from opportunities to obtain help? Why even raise these sorts of issues and questions?

To me, there are three very important reasons. The first is to underscore the point that although much human service progress has been made, a great deal of help continues to be needed. Second, raising these issues may help you find good reasons or causes to become involved and to exercise your creativity. Finally, consideration of how, why, and where human services are provided may help you identify a useful purpose for the efforts that you make on behalf of the people with whom you become involved.

To date, I have not found a general purpose, approach, or way of thinking about human services that works perfectly in all situations in which help is needed. One or another set of beliefs always seem to contain contradictions or limits. For example, I am obviously biased toward proactive behavioral treatment in community integrated settings, but I also recognize that some individuals who need help do not get to experience this sort of help. Perhaps it is unreasonable to expect that a general purpose for helping is possible, given the diversity of individual needs that exist, but that hasn't kept me from looking, and it probably shouldn't keep you from looking, either.

In retrospect, I have noticed that I have always viewed active treatment as if it were a law that I could not break. Being a law-abiding and rule-bound person, I have been quick to observe when it has not been present in a particular situation, and I have been driven to do a better job of attempting to provide it even when it was. When the idea that all help must be designed to produce greater personal autonomy or independence didn't seem broad enough for a particular situation, I admit that I have attempted to reinterpret and expand it to meet the need for help that seemed to exist at that place and time. As a result, I have sometimes described active treatment as an interaction between two persons that is intended to result in greater autonomy for one of the people. John Kirkpatrick and I (Softpath Habilitation, 1994) also described it as an interaction that consisted of five distinct components including being Positive, intervening Early when difficulties arise, with All people all the time, in a Reinforcing manner, while consistently Looking for opportunities to teach (PEARL). I refer to PEARL as a principle that directs people who provide assistance to do so in ways that invite greater individual independence or autonomy regardless of the context of the interaction (e.g., getting dressed, going to the bank, self-managing emotional behavior) and regardless of the current or ultimate level of performance that is expected in that context.

I now realize that I have been expanding the original concept of active treatment, which initially appeared in the literature of the HCFA, in order to encompass other contemporary helping themes, especially proactive treatment (e.g., inviting interaction). In addition, the newer language is intended to clearly strip away any boundaries related to *who* might be treated in these ways, *when* such interaction is relevant, and *where* it should be undertaken. In other words, you can interact in this way with *all* people (regardless of their current performance), *all* of the time (e.g., getting dressed, going to the bank), and in *all* places, regardless of current living situation or context in which you find yourself in a position to help. These assumptions probably existed in the literature all along. In my opinion, this is what makes the concept such an incredible way of describing and communicating the purpose of help.

If you are in a position to help someone put on his or her shoes, you are not providing active treatment if you simply put the shoes on his or her feet. This might be viewed as a nice thing to do, but it is unlikely to result in greater independence with respect to putting on shoes in the future. In fact, it may be likely to promote the individual's dependence on you as a caregiver. Of course, there are times when you will simply put on the shoes (e.g., because an individual is physically unable to participate, you are both in a hurry, you have been asked). If you are interested in providing active treatment, however, for some individuals, putting on shoes becomes a learning opportunity. Helping in ways that result in more independent putting on of shoes may result in learning, and learning may result in that individual having a few more choices and a little more quality in his or her life regardless of where he or she resides.

When you approach helping from an active treatment perspective, you can see how encompassing it can become and how much it can guide your potential helping actions. So many situations become potential learning opportunities: getting up in the morning, getting dressed, making breakfast, finding something to do, being with friends (or potential friends), playing a game, having fun, keeping a relationship, making a decision, changing the TV channel, solving a problem, communicating a need, dealing with an emotion, putting a worm on a hook, finding relaxation, securing enjoyment from work, knowing what to do in an emergency, and sleeping through the night can all become opportunities for you to help and opportunities for someone else to learn. For an individual in need of assistance with many aspects of living, active treatment can literally take place all day long. It doesn't need to be conducted in a special place or a special learning situation. The context in which you interact with the individual becomes the classroom, and you are a vital part of that context. The purpose is to help the individual function more independently within that context, ultimately with less and less of your help. It is just the right thing to do.

About 16 years ago, I was in a position to help at an institution for people who had been diagnosed as mentally ill or developmentally disabled, and sometimes both. On one living unit for people with particularly vivid challenges who did not communicate well verbally, the schedule for living was so tightly designed that the residents never had a moment of time to themselves to do anything they might have preferred to do. For many of the people providing assistance, this schedule looked very complete and very educational. Adults were escorted from one supervised "class" to another, to meals, to another class, and so on all day long until bedtime, which was at 8:30 P.M. for everyone. When I asked why the day was arranged this way, the people in a position to help simply stated that it worked. I think that what they meant was that it provided them with a way to arrange their job duties and create a routine that, if all went smoothly, looked good to their supervisors.

When asked if doing things this way created any greater independence or autonomy in the lives of the people who lived in this situation (i.e., was it consistent with the notion of active treatment?), in general the response was that it would help prepare these individuals for living more independently *if* they moved to the community. I didn't agree. I suggested that the schedule probably disregarded many individual preferences, taught dependence on others to arrange what life would or should look like, and provided almost no individual independence options from which people might learn. I reasoned that, if people were not provided opportunities to interact more independently within their living situation, then we could never know how well prepared they were to do so. I also suggested that living in the community usually included the expectation that there would be times (probably lots of them) when people would be expected to get along by themselves.

As a test, I asked the helpers if we could create a 1-hour block of time each morning at 11:00 A.M. for a scheduled activity that we would call *self-supervision*. (I figured if it was an hour long, fit into the existing schedule, and had a name, people might be more willing to give it a try.) During this time, we would increase free access to materials in the leisure areas on the unit, do our best *not* to give any instructions, provide positive verbal comments when people occupied themselves in safe ways, divert or redirect any problems that might arise, and track some of the things that people actually wound up doing.

The results of this little experiment helped contribute to the "half full or half empty" dilemma that I noted. Perhaps most important, the degree of disinterest from those in a position to help was remarkable. Some were actually so resistant to the idea of encouraging self-supervision that they threatened to file grievances to their union representatives and supervisors in the administration if the project proceeded. Others suggested that we could be breaking the law because it was our job to keep them busy. Still others just passively avoided participating. To this day, I am still uncertain as to why so many of them responded in these ways. Perhaps the request differed too much from other instructions they had received in the past (e.g., to avoid down time). Perhaps they were concerned that if the people in presumed need of assistance self-supervised too well, it could affect their jobs.

The effect on the people who lived on this unit was equally remarkable. On the first day that the hour was introduced, about 30 individuals converged in an open hallway from two different training rooms at 11:00 and received no instructions as to what they were supposed to do next. I like to imagine that for some of them, this might have been the first time they had ever been in such a situation. It was one of the most incredible situations I have ever observed.

For the longest time, everyone just stood there in the hallway. There was an extraordinary silence as if something had either gone terribly wrong or something amazing had just happened, but no one was quite sure. People just stood there in silence, waiting and waiting. Finally, after what seemed like a very long time, one or two of the individuals began to move away from the group very slowly, as if they were sneaking off. When the helpers resisted their temptation to instruct these people to stop, they gradually moved even a few steps farther away. More individuals began to move from the group. Several of them walked together very slowly down to the end of the long hallway and stood by an exit door from the unit. Did they think it was time for an outdoor activity? Were they communicating that perhaps it was a good time to have one? Others sat down on the floor in the hallway next to where some helpers were standing. Others began to move toward their rooms or other rooms where the doors were left open. Some people sat on their beds or began looking through whatever belongings were placed in their nightstands. Others began to interact with some of the new materials that were placed in the leisure area. In all, there was remarkably little interaction between people and an incredible silence. In retrospect, I now see that part of the reason it was so silent was that no instructions were being given.

Like so many different ways of doing things, the self-supervision hour gradually disappeared on this unit, and things eventually went back to the way they were. Perhaps everybody was more comfortable with this, but I never really believed so. As I look back, I realize that I probably did a very poor job of planning for change in this situation. I was not in a suitable mutually reinforcing relationship with the other potential helpers, and it is now crystal clear that I was expecting too much, too fast in this situation. I accidentally tipped the scales. I would do it much differently now.

For some helpers, the issue of who is in control can become a huge factor that influences the way they interact with others. A year or so later in a different place with different people, this point became particularly clear to me. Several of us were attempting to increase the interest, involvement, and productivity of a similar group of individuals within a vocational training situation. We were informed that this group was particularly difficult to keep involved and that they frequently wound up displaying behavior problems that resulted in the need to exclude them from the training room. Vocational tasks such as sorting or stapling were arranged, and participants were rewarded with praise, points, or little things to eat every 5 minutes or so if they remained at work and did not create any disruptions. This reinforcement strategy seemed reasonable, but it was only working at a certain level, and this was not generally viewed as being very good.

In this situation, a different idea was to teach participants to request the opportunity to receive the rewards if they preferred them and then gradually introduce the work expectations in between their requests and the delivery of the rewards. This seemed to be closely related to what most people do when they become involved in a work situation. Because the participants were mostly nonverbal, we decided that we would teach them to request rewards and work by pointing to or touching a big red X that we put up on the wall at the start of the sessions. We would interpret either of these actions as a request for a reinforcement opportunity. When people began to request without our assistance, the plan was to gradually begin to expect slightly more and more work prior to providing the praise, points, or little things to eat. We also taught people that they could request to be excused to a small area outside the room if they did not wish to participate. We thought this was more reasonable than having them behave dangerously in order to avoid participating.

Compared to the way things had been, the new approach produced a noticeable improvement in the group's productivity and desired behavior. Everyone quickly learned how to communicate their interest in receiving the rewards, and all but one person engaged in more of the work. That person usually requested to be excused after a short time. There were virtually no serious behavior problems, compared with the number of problems before the change. We were really excited about this, particularly because it seemed like this new way of giving control to these individuals really seemed to be enjoyable for them. In fact, on several occasions when we were doing things the old way (for sake of comparison), one young man would reach into my materials, take out the request board, and try to stick it up on the wall. We interpreted this as a clear indication of his preferences in the vocational training setting.

After our success in the vocational training situation, we began to use the different way in a leisure training setting as well with the same sort of positive results. When we attempted to introduce this more effective, enjoyable, and participant-preferred way of conducting training to the helpers in this program, however, a very interesting thing happened. Once again, they resisted doing things differently. In a meeting that we held in order to try to understand this resistance better, one of the most senior staff summarized his impression of the group's feelings clearly. He stated something like, "We are not going to do this. We are not here to respond to their requests. They are here to learn how to respond to ours."

Although I feel confident that my involvement as a helper in each of these situations probably produced some subtle changes in the way people interacted and may have had some impact on producing future programmatic changes, I would approach these situations more patiently and clearly now. In effect, I would proceed in a way very similar to the way the objectives have been outlined and presented in this book. For example, I would do my best to establish interactions with the staff that would not be likely to produce any harm for anyone in the situation. I would resist my natural inclination to blame or criticize any individual regardless of my opinions about their attitudes or behavior. I would look for reciprocity that existed in the interactions between myself and the staff, among individual staff members, and most important, between the program participants and the staff. I would do my best to increase the frequency of reinforce–reinforce reciprocal relationships between myself and the staff prior to suggesting or designing any changes in their program.

Once a more noticeable, mutually reinforcing relationship existed between myself and the staff, I would approach making program changes in much the same way I would approach devising an individual personal intervention plan. In other words, I would participate with the staff in discovering issues that were important or difficult for them, identifying ways that we could address them meaningfully together, and supporting their efforts. Of course, just as an effect of being present, I would introduce my personal thoughts and ideas into the situation and attempt to encourage particular desired behaviors using effective positive reinforcers. I would also do my best to bounce off any unpleasantness (e.g., staff upset, undermining, blatant resistance to change) that might arise along the way. Finally, I would gradually encourage staff to reconsider the purpose of their helping efforts in a way that was consistent with active treatment and find ways to experience and share the joy that can be derived from helping (see Objective Eight). In examining my own behavior over the years in those situations in which I believe my involvement made the most difference, it appears that these were the helping strategies that mattered the most.

SUMMARY

I think it is partially because of experiences like those noted in this objective that I have been inclined to respond very negatively to the word *compliance* when used in the context of a helping situation. I am not particularly interested in having people just do what I request. I am interested in helping people become more independent and autonomous in everything that *they* do. Although I recognize the potential value of some structured training situations, I am interested in helping whenever and wherever that help is needed—all day, any day, everywhere, and anywhere. I am interested in expanding the possible control that others have to communicate how they would prefer to have my help provided to them. I am listening as closely as possible to their desires and preferences because I am confident that, if I discover them, I will be in a better position to help. I want to help people have the outcomes that will empower them to have the highest quality of life that they can have. In my opinion, the purpose of help is something like that.

Experience the Joy of Helping

It is often apparent in helping situations that some helpers do not appear to be having a great deal of fun. These people seem to be the most prone to treating people poorly, promoting dependence, expecting compliance, frowning on different ways of doing things, and totally missing the point of establishing mutually reinforcing relationships with the people they are expected to help. These individuals also appear to incite the biggest behavior problems from people in need of assistance because of the manner in which they interact with them. In many ways, it appears that these people are stuck in attack–attack reciprocal relationships with the very individuals they are expected to assist. And life goes on? Maybe not, particularly if you put some of what you have learned into practice.

Although I have sometimes become so frustrated with people who attempt to help in coercive or forceful ways that I feel as though I can't resist my own natural inclination to attack, I have learned that doing so usually only makes matters worse. Remember that helpers never have an interest in making matters worse by doing harm to those they are attempting to assist. This should also guide your interactions with respect to those who may be in a position to help along with you. Do not blame them for acting the way that they do because this is likely to lead to greater frustration for you and less chance of actually changing the situation. Understand that there are reasons or causes for people's actions, even if you don't understand precisely what they are. You have also learned a thing or two about reciprocity, so you can predict that if you attack these people in some way (even by trying to ignore them), you are likely to prolong a difficult life situation.

Considering how people respond when a situation gets difficult, helpers have some choices. You may avoid or escape the difficulty, passively withdraw from it, get emotional (which is likely to make things worse), or find a way to make the situation better by getting to the source of the heat or difficulty. If you choose this latter, potentially productive way of responding, you are more likely to identify what situations are contributing to the difficulties, what it actually looks and feels like when they happen, what can be done instead, and what help you need from other helpers who may be involved in the situation to actually do those things you have identified. This may lead you to some success in helping those in need of help as well as those who might be in a position to help.

Yet, something is still missing. These concepts and ways of doing things may make sense, but what is going to drive the action? Why should you think and interact in these ways? Having had the opportunity to interact with and observe many wonderful helping teams, I am now convinced that there are at least two important reasons why you should consider these ideas. The first reason is that thinking about and interacting in these ways may make your difficult life situations less difficult than they have been. In other words, the *experience* of success in helping others in these ways may make certain parts of your life less difficult (e.g., if people are seeking your help in difficult situations, rather than displaying troublesome behaviors). As a result, your actions will be encouraged or reinforced, and you will be more likely to continue doing the things that contributed to that success. This is a very behavioral explanation.

The second reason is a little more difficult to describe in behavioral ways, but it is also based on the concept of reinforcement. As a result of thinking about and doing things in these ways, you may experience more frequent, more intense, or longer lasting *joy* from your participation in helping contexts. Once you have experienced this joy, you will be likely to continue thinking and interacting in the ways that are most likely to sustain it.

Increasing your sensitivity to actions that may produce harm, learning not to blame, experiencing reinforce–reinforce reciprocity, establishing mutually reinforcing relationships, teaching people to fish, bouncing off upsets, and conducting purposeful active treatment are all intended to be ways of interacting that make difficult situations less difficult *and* allow you to experience more of the joy of helping. How many times have you heard a person who provided some important help to someone else say something like, "I was more than happy to do it," or "I received a lot more than I ever gave," or "I'm just so glad I was able to help"? How many times have you seen the glow in the helper's eyes, the bounce in his step, the smile on her face? How many times have you been in circumstances that have allowed you to say or show these things?

Consider for a moment what it would be like to experience less pain from difficult life situations, greater success in your helping interactions, and more joy from having the opportunity to participate in the life of someone you are attempting to help. Hopefully, the notions of less pain and greater success are generally attractive. But how does this concept of joy work in relation to your organizational leaders and administrators who sometimes appear to be concerned only with the cost of helping? How important is it to those co-workers who are only at their current job because they couldn't find anything else to do? How can it be presented to other potential helpers who seem to believe that learning must be forced on people and who pressure you to do things like they do? Most important of all, how willing are you to consider, accept, discuss, and even seek out this joy?

As it turns out, the last several years of my professional life have given me many special opportunities to attempt to assist potential helpers to do a better job of helping. In the process, I have begun to believe that when my thoughts or actions have an impact on the helpers, then ultimately I am providing help to greater numbers of people. To me, that seems like a reasonable explanation for some of my own behavior. But lately, I have been wondering if there isn't really a little more to this change in my behavior.

As I thought more about it, it seemed that I have always wondered about who was actually in more need of help: the young man I encountered in the Army or the specialists; the person with the brain injury or those who have unreasonable expectations of him; Gerry, the adolescent who pulled hair or those of us who treated him in the way that we did, the very needy individuals in all of the programs or the people who were employed to assist them, myself or the people I find myself interacting with?

Then something occurred to me. It really wasn't that one group of people needed help more than another. It wasn't about this person helping that person or that person helping someone else. It was not even about the kind of help that a particular individual needed. It was in this thing that we all seem to share— the need for help. *Not one person is actually in a position to handle his or her most difficult life situations without involvement or interaction with others.*

This can be a very exciting realization that may focus your attention on how everyone is alike rather than how we are different. I think this is why mutual reinforcement is such a remarkable concept that could actually guide what everyone seems to be striving for. If people are together, then there is much less likelihood that we will be apart, alone, disenfranchised, sad, angry, frustrated, or attacked. These experiences are what I have always wanted in my life, a sense of connectedness with everybody else, the chance to participate, and the opportunity to give and receive help. There can be very special joy from helping, and everyone may need more practice at sharing it.

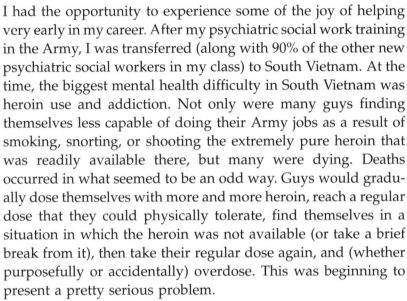

I had the opportunity to experience some of the joy of helping very early in my career. After my psychiatric social work training in the Army, I was transferred (along with 90% of the other new psychiatric social workers in my class) to South Vietnam. At the time, the biggest mental health difficulty in South Vietnam was heroin use and addiction. Not only were many guys finding themselves less capable of doing their Army jobs as a result of smoking, snorting, or shooting the extremely pure heroin that was readily available there, but many were dying. Deaths occurred in what seemed to be an odd way. Guys would gradu-ally dose themselves with more and more heroin, reach a regular dose that they could physically tolerate, find themselves in a situation in which the heroin was not available (or take a brief break from it), then take their regular dose again, and (whether purposefully or accidentally) overdose. This was beginning to present a pretty serious problem.

As part of the military's attempt to alleviate this problem, my classmates and I were stationed at various drug amnesty centers in different parts of the country. The Army permitted soldiers who confessed to using heroin to admit themselves to these centers for 14 days without military or legal consequences in order to "dry out." Very many of them did.

There were stories of joy and sadness in this experience, but one was particularly important to me. Doug, a bright red-headed kid, checked in. Although Doug certainly looked the part of the infantry grunt, his beads, faded uniform, and boonie hat didn't hide his silence and noticeable isolation from the rest of the guys who checked in with him. Also, as everybody else in his group was going through physical withdrawal from their heroin use, Doug seemed to be in no particular distress. We knew that something else was going on with Doug, and we also knew that when we got his drug test results back (which were negative for heroin), he would be out of the center as quickly as he came. We had about 24 hours to provide whatever help he needed.

Doug and I connected very quickly, maybe because I had initiated an effort or maybe because we were from the same home state. After establishing a reciprocal relationship with him as quickly as possible, I felt I would produce no harm by letting him in on what the rest of us already knew—that he was not addicted to heroin and that he would have to return up-country to his infantry unit much earlier than the expected 14 days. Doug seemed to know that this was coming. There we sat, in the very dark middle of a night in which the quiet was broken only by the sound of distant artillery and nearby vomiting.

Before the sun came up, I felt like I had learned what Doug needed to teach me about himself: his intense fear of dying; his broken love relationship back home; his sense that his life would be worth much more at some point in the future; and his very deep sense of loneliness, despair, and not belonging. I had also shared a good deal about my own experience that wasn't all that different from his at that time of my life. We connected, but unfortunately we both knew there was a clock ticking away the moments before some kind of decision would need to be made. What was Doug going to do?

He could return to the unit and possibly die like he feared. He could take one big dose of heroin and possibly avoid the whole thing. He could refuse to get on the truck that would take him from his firebase unit back to the bush. He could wind up in military prison for having thoughts and feelings that he was willing to share when so many others didn't or couldn't. I remember being very scared. I knew that I couldn't advise him to take one action or another because all of the options seemed to have potentially terrible outcomes.

We never reached a decision that dawn about what Doug was going to do. We just agreed that he was a very special person and that when the time came, he would take whatever action presented itself, and it would be the right action to take. Actually, this was a powerful conclusion to a very long night for both of us. He walked away to the barracks, and I walked away for coffee.

About mid-morning, people from his unit had already heard that Doug's drug test was clean, and a big steel "deuce and a half" truck showed up at our gate to pick him up. I saw him walking up the drive, and I'm sure he saw me, but there was no real eye contact. In that moment, I am sure that both of us had feelings that were unique and indescribable. I had an intense fear that I had not helped. I was not comforted by the thought that I had done my military duty to get this soldier back to his unit. I don't remember saying a word to anyone as the truck pulled off with Doug sitting alone on one of the bench seats in the back. I do remember having silent eye contact with a couple of my fellow psychiatric social workers, who seemed to know exactly what was up. For the next few days, there was an incredible sense of fear and apprehension around the amnesty center. Instead of looking at the morning report like we always did, with the hope that none of our guys had overdosed, everyone avoided it. And then it happened.

Just as we were when Doug had pulled away a few days earlier, most of us happened to be standing out front when he returned. We watched him jump from the back of the truck, grab his pack and M-16 rifle (which were both loaded for the bush), and run in our direction. He was smiling from ear to ear and looking toward the sky as he ran. When he got to me, he dropped all his stuff and held me for what seemed like an eternity. Everyone was laughing and shouting and carrying on in what was clearly one of our most special moments of joy. This feeling didn't change even when we learned that Doug had abandoned his unit the previous afternoon. After all, as Doug kept saying over and over through his smile, "I'm alive." We shared our joy long into that night.

I describe this memory of Doug and my fellow helpers in Vietnam for a couple reasons. In order to experience the joy that is available from participating with others in a helping relationship, you have to develop the skill of observing yourself when it is happening. This part of helping is not about producing any particular outcome other than what appears to matter most to the person you are attempting to assist. Doug felt that he had made the most important decision of his life. It obviously brought him great joy at that moment, and his actions were a clear indication that he wished to share it with those he felt had helped produce it. The joy, or the sense of connectedness with other human beings, is likely to be what keeps you coming back to helping. I have participated in the production of a lot of results in my life, but none have been as important and reinforcing of my own efforts to help as the experience of joy that I have had because of those moments of connectedness with others. I am no longer embarrassed or shy about declaring that I would like to have as many of those moments as I can get because I believe that they are helpful for me. I have seen them be helpful for others as well.

I am also convinced that learning how to experience the joy that comes from helping can be a very important skill for people who find themselves in a position to help. To me, it is not surprising that people who seem to get the least joy from helping are the same people who really don't seem to be very good at it. Observe yourself. When the experience of joy shows up for you, allow yourself to have it. Explore the causes or the reasons why you are having it. Recognize that the mutually reinforcing (and productive) relationship you have developed with the person in need of help is the source and the context for the feeling *and* whatever results are produced. You interacted in a way that put you in a position to help. Congratulate yourself. Don't ever apologize to those who would have you see it differently.

The second reason I describe my memory of Doug is because I believe it is important to learn how to communicate and share the joy that you receive from helping. For example, if you can potentially help one individual and you are not in contact with others, you might learn to share your joy with the person you are assisting. Let them know somehow when those moments are special to you. The reason for this is that it may take the heat off them (if they are feeling bad about needing help) or strengthen the very behaviors that produce that feeling for you.

It may be more of an exercise to share the joy if you are in a position to help with others who are in the same role. Sometimes the joy seems to go out of these situations. This is when the extent of the problems that people are facing may overwhelm any sense of joy that anyone is experiencing. Or it may be because one or several individuals seem to discourage such expressions. These people may view it as a sign of your lack of maturity, secondary to their perception of the purpose of the work, or just plain silly. In my opinion, it is more likely that these individuals are either not observing themselves very closely for their own joy, have a difficult time expressing it, or believe that they are being encouraged by others to keep it to themselves. They could also believe that allowing themselves to observe or express it more clearly will make them feel more connected to certain people than they wish to be. Your job in this situation is to help them get over it. It is important for them to get over it because their lack of expression may discourage it in others, and it is very possible that they may become better helpers if they allow themselves to experience some of the joy. Create a context for them to express it, point it out to them when you observe it in their actions, and publicly acknowledge their little bits of excitement when you see them. Soon, you will be doing it together. This is a different sort of reciprocity and mutual rein-forcement among those who provide the help. Don't let the tough guys make the rules. Experience the joy!

On Beliefs, Science, and Getting Ready to Help

At times in this little book, I have made some attempt to use certain words carefully (e.g., I believe, in my opinion). I suppose this is because I view words as representations of an individual's perceptions of the relationships among emotions, events, and other things and not necessarily truths. I also learned somewhere along the line that if you didn't have particular kinds of facts, data, or authority to support the words you used or the beliefs you had, then you are probably better off not trying to communicate them. So, for the sake of those people who taught me, I have actually noticed myself being cautious.

I suppose that I really don't have any conventional data to support much of what I have said here. I have tried to introduce scientific techniques by accentuating certain concepts such as observing, testing relationships, and predicting results. I could find some more support in theory and present more conventional data that would relate to many things that I have communicated.

But I fear that if I did that, I would not have had one of my most desired results. Many potential helpers probably would not have read the book.

Yet, perhaps these beliefs are just a matter of my perception. If so, then my perception probably results from observing my experience of what has worked in many different situations. My hope is that the words that I have used to describe these perceptions can change behavior. My belief is that if you act in ways that are consistent with what has been communicated here, you will experience success and joy in situations in which you can help someone. That is what happened for me. If I didn't believe those things, I wouldn't have communicated them. I wish you great success, joy, and even a sense of connectedness on your way.

Bibliography

□ □ □ □ □ □

Americans with Disabilities Act (ADA) of 1990, PL 101-336, 42 U.S.C. §§ 12101 *et seq.*

Azrin, N.H. (1978, February). A strategy for applied research: Learning based but outcome oriented. *The American Psychologist,* 140–149.

Carr, E.G., & Durand, V.M. (1985). Reducing behavior problems through functional communication training. *Journal of Applied Behavior Analysis, 18,* 111–126.

Carr, E.G., Levin, L., McConnachie, G., Carlson, J.I., Kemp, D.C., & Smith, C.E. (1994). *Communication-based intervention for problem behavior: A user's guide for producing positive change.* Baltimore: Paul H. Brookes Publishing Co.

Condeluci, A. (1991). *Interdependence: The route to community.* Boca Raton, FL: CRC Press.

D'Zurilla, T.J., & Goldfried, M.R. (1971). Problem solving and behavior modification. *Journal of Abnormal Psychology, 78,* 107–126.

Education for All Handicapped Children Act of 1975, PL 94-142, 20 U.S.C. §§ 1400 *et seq.*

Holland, J.G. (1978). Behaviorism: Part of the problem or part of the solution? *Journal of Applied Behavior Analysis, 11,* 163–174.

Kauffman, J.M. (Ed.). (1981). Special Issue: Are all children educable? *Analysis and intervention in developmental disabilities* (Volume 1). New York: Pergamon Press.

Kazdin, A.E. (1975). *Behavior modification in applied settings.* Homewood, IL: The Dorsey Press.

Koegel, L.K., Koegel, R.L., & Dunlap, G. (1996). *Positive behavioral support: Including people with difficult behavior in the community.* Baltimore: Paul H. Brookes Publishing Co.

Lovett, H. (1996). *Learning to listen: Positive approaches and people with difficult behavior.* Baltimore: Paul H. Brookes Publishing Co.

Mahoney, M.J., & Thoresen, C.E. (1974). *Self-control: Power to the person.* Monterey, CA: Brooks/Cole Publishing Co.

McMorrow, M.J. (1994). Toward proactive treatment of serious unwanted behavior following acquired brain injury. *i.e. Magazine, 2,* 14–21.

McMorrow, M.J. (1997). Personal intervention: A compensatory strategy for self-management of emotional behavior. In K. Fralish & M.J. McMorrow (Eds.), *Innovations in brain injury rehabilitation* (pp. 1–27), New York: Ahab Press.

Skinner, B.F. (1971). *Beyond freedom and dignity.* New York: Bantam/Vintage Books.

Skinner, B.F. (1976). *About behaviorism.* New York: Bantam/Vintage Books.

Softpath Habilitation. (1994). *Active treatment with PEARL.* Available from Softpath Habilitation. Box 540, Cobden, IL 62920.

Trumbo, D. (1984). *Johnny got his gun.* New York: Bantam/Vintage Books. (Original work published 1934)